PROBLEM SOLVING
Critical Thinking and Communication Skills

PROBLEM SOLVING
Critical Thinking and Communication Skills

Linda W. Little
Ingrid A. Greenberg

Longman

Problem Solving: Critical Thinking and Communication Skills

Longman, 95 Church Street, White Plains, N.Y. 10601

Associated companies:
Longman Group Ltd., London
Longman Cheshire Pty., Melbourne
Longman Paul Pty., Auckland
Copp Clark Pitman, Toronto

Distributed in the United Kingdom by Longman Group
Ltd., Longman House, Burnt Mill, Harlow, Essex CM20
2JE, England and by associated companies, branches,
and representatives throughout the world.

Executive editor: Joanne Dresner
Development editor: Debbie Sistino
Production editor: Helen B. Ambrosio
Text design: Pencil Point Studio
Cover design: Anne M. Pompeo
Text art: Leslie Dunlap/Publishers' Graphics, Inc.
Production supervisor: Anne Armeny

Library of Congress Cataloging in Publication Data
Little, Linda W. (Linda Waltraub)
    Problem solving: critical thinking and communication
skills / by Linda W. Little, Ingrid A. Greenberg.
        p.   cm.
ISBN 0-8013-0603-5
    1. English language—Textbooks for foreign speakers. 2. Critical
thinking. 3. Communication. I. Greenberg, Ingrid A. II. Title.
PE1128.L496   1991
428.2'4—dc20
                                                            90-45184
                                                            CIP

6 7 8 9 10-CRS-99

CONTENTS

INTRODUCTION

THE IMPORTANCE OF PROBLEM SOLVING

Many refugees and immigrants to the United States have difficulty adjusting to their new country and its culture. They arrive with personal and economic expectations that are often not met, and find it difficult to mesh their own values and beliefs with those of their new country. This culture shock is further compounded for those individuals who were forced to leave their countries, who left family members behind and who have no means of supporting themselves. All these problems can interfere with the learning process.

The Brazilian educator Paulo Freire suggests that by discussing the students' problems and concerns in class, some of this interference to learning can be relieved. Through problem solving, students learn to analyze and think critically about a problem, examine its causes, identify some possible solutions and their consequences and then decide on an action.

While talking about problems in ESL classes, students use the target language and improve their communicative skills. As they discuss the implications of the problems and share their experiences and beliefs, they learn more about the target culture and the cultural beliefs of others. They learn to interact with others as they discuss solutions and consequences of solutions. They learn to negotiate as they try to agree upon a possible solution. As students practice this in class, they develop their critical thinking skills and they learn a process which can help them cope with future problems.

ORGANIZATION

The problem-solving stories and dialogues in this book are based on the problems and experiences that the students in our ESL classes have shared with us. The book is organized into six topical units: the family, housing, money, transportation, health and pre-employment problems. This order parallels the life skills units in most ESL curricula and basic core texts. However, the problems and units are not dependent on each other and may be used in any order. To facilitate teacher and student use of this book, the format and the directions have been kept simple and consistent. Each unit contains three fully-developed problems (problems followed by exercises). At the end of each unit are additional problems that can be developed and used in class. The emphasis in this book is on communication, cultural comparisons, higher order thinking and decision-making skills. All language skills, listening, speaking, reading and writing are part of the process. The instructional delivery is varied within each problem and includes whole class, group, pair and individual activities.

INSTRUCTOR'S AND STUDENTS' ROLES

In *Problem Solving*, the instructor introduces problems that are of concern to the students and acts as a facilitator who guides the discussion while the students actively contribute to their own learning process. It is a learner-centered, communicative process where the students interact with each other in order to examine problems and make choices and decisions for possible future actions. When necessary, the instructor also acts as a cultural informant and language expert helping the students say what they wish to say. This helps the students develop the cultural awareness and communicative language skills needed to take some actions in solving their problems.

ERROR CORRECTION

In order for problem solving to work effectively in a classroom situation, we suggest that the theories of Stephen Krashen and Tracy Terrell and the general principles of the Natural Approach be followed. It is important to provide a relaxed atmosphere in which students will not be embarrassed or intimidated. Be sensitive to the students' feelings and respect students' wishes to speak or to remain silent. Since problem solving is a communicative activity, the emphasis is on the message (what the student is saying) and not on the grammatical form (how the student is saying it). As long as the message is clear, the students' grammar need not be corrected, because correction may discouage the student, who will be reluctant to express his or her ideas.

Grammar can be covered in follow-up activities the next day. By observing the students during discussions and making note of errors, any future instruction can address these needs. Thus the grammar that is taught grows out of a need to use it, and students, seeing the need are more motivated to learn.

USING PROBLEM SOLVING

Prereading

The prereading discussion is meant to motivate the students to read the story or dialogue. The questions set the context for the reading and give students a chance to predict or guess what the problem might be. Students should be looking at the illustration in their books as the prereading questions are asked. If an overhead projector is available, the picture could be projected on a wall or screen. Lower level students may simply describe the picture, while higher level students will focus more on the situation conveyed in the picture. The questions encourage vocabulary development and the exchange of ideas. Feel free to pose additional questions based on the level, needs and interest of the class.

Reading the Story or Dialogue

The students first read the story or dialogue silently. They should underline words that they don't understand rather than use their dictionaries. It is important for students to begin to get meaning from context. Circulate around the classroom and find out which words the students don't understand. Write these words on the board. Then read the story aloud to the students and ask the students to listen and follow along. When reading a dialogue, show that there are two parts. Either ask a volunteer student to help read, or read both parts by switching places or changing the pitch of your voice. Hearing the story also makes it possible for lower level students to understand the story and participate in the problem-solving discussion that follows. After reading the story or dialogue, ask the students to look at the words on the board. Ask the class questions about the meanings of the words as they relate to the story.

Comprehension Check

The comprehension check can be done as a listening or as a reading exercise.

Listening

Students should have their books closed. Read each sentence aloud and ask the students to answer yes, no or maybe. They can respond orally by simply calling out the answer, or silently by using hand signals (thumbs up for yes, thumbs down for no and an open wavering hand for maybe). Note that hand signals mean different things in different cultures, so before using this method in class check with your students. An alternative to using hand signals is for students to hold up cards that say yes, no or maybe. When students respond orally, they sometimes say whatever they hear the loudest. Responding silently, with hand signals or cards, requires students to think a little harder before committing to an answer.

Reading

Students read the sentences silently and write the answers next to the sentences. Volunteers can then read each sentence aloud as the whole class answers. If any of the answers spark debate, encourage students to go back to the reading and find the sentences that support their answer.

Variation

Pair students. S1 has his or her book closed while S2 reads the first five statements. S1 responds orally and S2 records the answers. Have them switch roles for sentences 6 through 10. This is good listening and clarification practice. If the student that is listening does not understand a statement, requests to repeat or clarify must be made. Circulate around the classroom and make note of any pronunciation problems or other difficulties.

What's Happening?

This section includes concrete *Wh-* questions. All the answers to the questions can be found in the reading. This section is designed to be done orally first and then as a written exercise.

After discussing the answers orally, review the questions with the students. Ask them to write the answers in complete sentences. Ask volunteers to write the answers on the board. Correct the sentences on the board together, giving students a chance to make corrections on their own papers. Encourage the students to refer to the reading whenever there is uncertainty about the answer.

Variation

Have the students ask each other the questions in pairs. The student who is listening should not look at the questions. This is good oral practice and gives students an opportunity to ask clarification questions.

Talk It Over

This section is meant to promote discussion among the students. It encourages students to talk about issues presented in the reading and also about their personal experiences. Many questions ask about the students' experience with practical aspects of life such as banking and health insurance. These life-skills questions are an effective way for students to obtain practical information and learn from the experiences of others.

Other questions require students to make inferences and use their judgement. There are no right or wrong answers. It is a good idea to preview these questions before using them in class as there may be an occasional question that is not appropriate for your class or might embarrass someone. There may also be some new vocabulary in this section that needs to be clarified.

Frequently, questions require students to compare and contrast their cultures with the United States. If several countries or cultures are represented in the class, a simple chart can be drawn on the board and students from each country can give answers. The chart can illustrate how U.S. culture differs from the students' native cultures. The goal is to make students more aware of the target culture and the cultural beliefs of others. Insights into U.S. culture can be offered, but care must be taken not to over simplify or stereotype. Cultural acceptance cannot be forced, but an understanding of other cultures often promotes tolerance and acceptance.

What's the Problem?

This section is the heart of *Problem Solving*. By this point the students are familiar with the story and the issues surrounding it. The class is ready to identify the problem(s), find solutions and talk about the consequences. This section guides students through the process of identifying the problem(s) in the reading, choosing some solutions and discussing the consequences of each solution.

Ask the students what the problems are in the story. List the problems on the chalkboard. The class might identify only one problem or they might find many. We have seen different classes find very different problems within the same story. It largely depends on whatever the students are experiencing in their own lives.

The class will choose the one problem it wants to discuss. Circle the problem the majority chooses. (If there is a split, discuss one of the problems on one day and the other problem the next day.)

Start the discussion by asking, "What's the problem?" then, "What can be done about the problem?" and "What is the solution to the problem?" The students volunteer ideas. The emphasis is on ideas, not on grammar. Do not correct students. Help them if they are struggling. Occasionally, students cannot think of anything to say. Give them some time to think, be patient and ask some leading questions such as, "Who is unhappy?" "Who has a problem?" "Why does this person feel this way?" "Have you ever felt that way?" "When?" "What happened?" "What did you do?" When solutions are offered, write them on the board. Then turn the students' attention to consequences. Ask the students, "What will happen if so-and-so does such-and-such?" Encourage them to use their imaginations, their experience with this problem and critical thinking skills to come up with some consequences. List the consequences next to each solution on the board.

To choose the "best" solution, put the students into groups. The task is to find a solution or a number of solutions and to discuss the consequences. Then, if possible, to choose one solution that is best.

This group activity gives quiet students a chance to speak up. It may help a student that was intimidated to offer an idea in front of the whole class. Students may think of new solutions too. Appoint a leader in each group that will act as facilitator and write down the solution. Circulate around the classroom and ask students what solutions they have chosen. Give them encouragement and positive feedback. Make note of the difficulties they have in expressing themselves. These can be covered the next day.

When the groups have arrived at a solution, ask the leader of each group to tell the class the solution and why it was chosen. List the solutions on the board. Then see if the class can agree on one solution. This may or may not be possible, but it will give the students a chance to persuade others of their viewpoint.

After students have been through a few units, it may not be necessary to guide them through the process. They can complete this section in groups. It is best if students in each group are from different countries, speak different languages and are of different ages and sex. This will ensure that English is used and that many diverse viewpoints are brought into the discussion. The groups can discuss the solutions and consequences and report their conclusions to the class.

What Would You Do?

Ask each student to write down his or her particular solution and reasons why he or she feels this is the best solution. This section is meant to give every student in class a chance to state his or her opinion. This is a final chance for students to express what they really think. Some might have had completely different solutions, but might not have had the courage to speak up in class. Collect the papers and comment only on the content, not on the grammar. Return the papers to the students. Note any difficulties students have in expressing themselves. Future instruction can be geared to these particular difficulties.

Speak Up!

Very often students feel they know what the solution to a problem is, but if it entails speaking to a person of the target culture, they are at a loss. Generating appropriate language to solve the problem is a challenge for most students. They know what they want to say, but they don't have the functional language skills needed to say it. For example, students have identified the problem and task below:

Problem identified: Juan did not get paid for overtime hours.

Students' decision: Juan should ask for his money.

Task: Create a dialogue asking for the money without making the boss angry.

Ask the class, "What can Juan say to his boss?" Write the students' suggestions on the board. For example, a student may volunteer, "You no pay me money. I work hard for you." After several suggestions have been made, ask the students which version they like best and why they liked it. Ask them what changes they would make in the other versions and why they would change them. It is best if the students can identify the reasons for changing the dialogue. Ask the students, "What will the boss think if Juan talks to him like this?" After some changes and editing, the new version might look something like this: "Excuse me, is this right? I think I got paid for only five days last week, but I worked six days." Discuss the employer's reaction to this version and ask the students which version is best. Ask volunteers to role play the situation.

Small Groups and Pairs

More advanced students can work in small groups or pairs. They create a dialogue, write it down, and present it to the class. The class provides feedback in the same manner as mentioned above.

Share Your Ideas

This section is different for every story since these exercises are meant to provide follow-up to the issues found in the story. These exercises are life-skills oriented and directions are provided.

ACKNOWLEDGMENTS

We would like to thank our students for sharing their personal experiences and family histories with us. Without our students' trust and their input, this book would not have been possible. We are grateful to all the teachers who have shared students' problems with us at workshops and seminars. Some of the lessons in this book are based on stories obtained at those meetings.

We deeply appreciate Joanne Dresner's interest in our project. Special thanks go to Debbie Sistino, who provided invaluable editing advice and offered feedback during every stage of the book. It was a pleasure to work with Debbie and the Longman Publishing Group.

We would also like to thank K. Lynn Savage, Leanne Howard, Gretchen Bitterlin and Laurie Gifford for their encouragement and support and Ruth Rominger for her editing advice and valuable feedback.

Dedicated to my mother Paula R. Stang who has always been there when I needed her.

L.W.L.

Dedicated to my parents, Mary and Sanford, who I look to for inspiration.
In memory of a very special friend, Scott I. Hillman.

I.A.G.

1. LANE'S PROBLEM

What do you see in the picture?

Who is on the bench?

Is he with a friend?

How does he feel?

What are the people in the picture doing?

Read the story silently. Underline words you don't understand. Your teacher will help you with new words.

When Lane came to the United States seven years ago, he went to English classes and studied hard. He also got some training in welding. Then he got a good job with a big company. Lane has been working there for the last four years. His pay is very good and he saves a lot of his money. He should feel happy, but he is sad and lonely.

It's Sunday again. He hates Sundays. He went to the beach alone and watched the happy families have fun. Then he went to a restaurant alone and watched many young couples enjoying their meals. After that he went to a movie and felt lonely again. Now he is alone at home.

Lane is 35 years old. His parents and brothers and sisters are still in his country. He misses them. He wants to have a wife and children. Some of his friends go to bars and meet women there, but Lane does not like to drink. In his country parents help sons find good wives. Who can help him here? Where can he meet a nice woman in the United States?

A. COMPREHENSION CHECK.

Listen to your teacher read the sentences and answer yes, no or maybe.

1. Lane is 35 years old and single.
2. His family lives in the United States.
3. He just got a job.
4. He is a hard worker.
5. He has saved a lot of money.
6. Lane enjoys his weekends.
7. He likes to go to bars and drink.
8. He is sad and lonely on Sundays.
9. He has an American girlfriend.
10. He wants to get married.

B. WHAT'S HAPPENING?

First answer the questions orally. Then write down the answers.

1. How long has Lane been in the United States?

   _____

2. What kind of training does he have?

   _____

3. When did he start working for his company?

   _____

4. Does he spend all his money?

   _____

5. Where is Lane's family?

   _____

6. What does Lane do on weekends?

   _____

7. Why is Lane so sad on Sundays?

   _____

8. What do Lane's friends like to do?

_____

9. Why doesn't Lane go out to bars with his friends?

_____

10. What is Lane looking for?

_____

11. How do men find wives in Lane's native country?

_____

C. TALK IT OVER.

Discuss the questions with your teacher and classmates. Talk about your personal experiences. Compare your country and the United States. What is the same? What is different?

1. Are you married? Did you live at home with your parents before you got married? How old were you when you got married?

2. Where do most young people in your country live before they get married? Why? Is it the same or different in the United States? Why?

3. Do young people in your country spend more time with their families or with their friends before they get married? Why? Is it the same in the United States? Why? Why not?

4. Do you think young people enjoy themselves more in your country or in the United States? What do they do in their free time?

5. Where did you meet your husband or wife (boyfriend or girlfriend)? Where do most people in your country meet someone to marry? Where do people in the United States meet their future husbands or wives?

6. Do you think people are more lonely in your country or in the United States? Why?

7. Do you feel sad and lonely sometimes? When? Are you lonelier during the week or on weekends? Why?

8. What do you do when you feel sad and lonely?

9. If you are not married, and you don't live with your family, what can you do so that you are not lonely?

10. Are only single people lonely? Do people who live with their families get lonely too? When? Why?

11. Do you think Lane will make a good husband? Why? Why not?

D. WHAT'S THE PROBLEM?

Tell your teacher all the problems in the story. Your teacher will list the problems on the chalkboard.

With your classmates, choose one problem you want to discuss today. Write down the problem.

_____

_____

Find some solutions to this problem. Talk about the consequences of each solution.

What can be done about the problem? Write down some possible solutions.

1. _____

_____

2. _____

_____

3. _____

_____

What might happen if you do that? Write down a possible consequence of each solution.

1. _____

_____

2. _____

_____

3. _____

_____

In small groups, discuss the solutions and consequences. Choose the one solution you think is best. Each group should share its solution with the class. Tell your teacher and classmates why you think this is the best solution. Can your class agree on one solution?

E. WHAT WOULD YOU DO?

Help Lane. You are his friend. Give him some advice. Tell Lane what to do. Write down what you would say to him.

Lane, I think you should _____

_____

_____

F. SPEAK UP!

Work in small groups or with a partner. Choose someone that Lane should talk to. Should he talk to his friends, a young woman at the park or somebody else? What should he say? Write a conversation that might help Lane.

Lane: _____

_____ : _____

Lane: _____

_____ : _____

Lane: _____

_____ : _____

G. SHARE YOUR IDEAS.

You are looking for a wife or a husband (or boyfriend or girlfriend). What is most important to you? Look at the list below. Number the list, starting with number 1, in the order of what is most important to you. Add your own ideas to the list.

My _____ has to . . .
(wife/husband/boyfriend/girlfriend)

be a nonsmoker	have the same religion as me	be about my age
be healthy	respect me	be very clean
love me	speak my language	
understand me	be a good cook	
be rich	be a good dancer	_____
love children	have a good job	
be good-looking	be honest	_____
have a good education	know how to fix things	
come from my country	be careful with money	_____
be strong	get along with my family	
come from a good family	like my friends	_____

Share your answers with your classmates. Tell them why some things are very important to you and why other things are not very important to you.

2. MARIA'S PROBLEM

What do you see in the picture?

What is the young woman doing?

What is she thinking about?

How does she feel?

Read the story silently. Underline words you don't understand. Your teacher will help you with new words.

Maria Garcia is the youngest of six children. Her family came to the United States six years ago. Her parents work very hard, but they don't have a lot of money.

Maria will finish high school in June. She will be the first person in her family to graduate from high school. She is an excellent student. She won a four-year scholarship to a college in another state. Her family is very happy and proud of her. They want Maria to go to college. They are glad that the scholarship will pay for her education.

Maria wants to go to college too, but she has a problem. She is in love. Her boyfriend Toni does not want her to go away for four years. He is 27 and he wants to get married now. He has a good full-time job with benefits in a factory. He wants to have a wife and family. He says he will take care of Maria and she doesn't need a college education or a job. Maria doesn't know what to do.

A. COMPREHENSION CHECK.

Listen to your teacher read the sentences and answer yes, no or maybe.

1. Maria comes from a large family.
2. Maria's family has plenty of money.
3. Maria is a very good student.
4. Her family will pay for her college education.
5. She has a scholarship at a college in her city.
6. Maria's family wants her to go to college.
7. Maria's boyfriend Toni wants her to go to college.
8. Toni has a good job in a factory.
9. Toni wants his wife to work.
10. Maria loves Toni, but she also wants to go to college.

B. WHAT'S HAPPENING?

First answer the questions orally. Then write down the answers.

1. How long has Maria's family been in the United States?

   _____

2. How many brothers and sisters does Maria have?

   _____

3. Who will pay for Maria's college education?

   _____

4. Is the scholarship from a college near Maria's hometown?

   _____

5. For how many years will Maria have to go away to college?

   _____

6. Does Maria want to go to college?

   _____

(Continued on next page.)

7. Who is Toni?

_____

8. How does Maria feel about Toni?

_____

9. Why doesn't Toni want Maria to go to college?

_____

C. TALK IT OVER.

Discuss the questions with your teacher and classmates. Talk about your personal experiences. Compare your country and the United States. What is the same? What is different?

1. Did you go to school or college in your country? Did anybody in your family go to high school or college?

2. How many years did your parents go to school?

3. Do you have to get a good education in your country so that you can get a good job?

4. Is education free in your country or do you have to pay for it? Is it expensive?

5. How many years do most men go to school in your country? How many years do most women go to school in your country?

6. Who gets a better education in your country, men or women? Why?

7. How many years do people in the United States go to school?

8. What do young, unmarried women do in your country? Do they work, go to school or stay home? What do they do in the United States?

9. Do many women work outside the home in your country? In the United States? Which women work outside the home most in your country: young single women, married women, women with children, women with no children, widows, divorced women, poor women, rich women, old women? What about in the United States?

10. What happens to a family in your country if the husband loses his job, gets sick, divorces his wife or dies? What do you think happens to a family in the United States?

11. Do you want your children to finish high school and go to college? Why? Why not?

12. Do you think it is important that young men and women get a good education in the United States? Why? Why not?

13. Why do Maria's parents want her to go to college?

D. WHAT'S THE PROBLEM?

Tell your teacher all the problems in the story. Your teacher will list the problems on the chalkboard.

With your classmates, choose one problem you want to discuss today. Write down the problem.

_____

_____

Find some solutions to this problem. Talk about the consequences of each solution.

What can be done about the problem? Write down some possible solutions.	What might happen if you do that? Write down a possible consequence of each solution.
1. _____	1. _____
2. _____	2. _____
3. _____	3. _____

In small groups, discuss the solutions and consequences. Choose the one solution you think is best. Each group should share its solution with the class. Tell your teacher and classmates why you think this is the best solution. Can your class agree on one solution?

E. WHAT WOULD YOU DO?

Help Maria. You are her friend. Give her some advice. Tell Maria what to do. Write down what you would say to her.

Maria, I think you should _____

_____

_____

F. SPEAK UP!

Work in a small group or with a partner. Choose someone that Maria should talk to. Should she talk to Toni, her parents, her brother, her sister, a counselor or somebody else? What should she say? Write a conversation that might help Maria.

Maria: _____

_____ : _____

Maria: _____

_____ : _____

Maria: _____

_____ : _____

G. SHARE YOUR IDEAS.

What do you think young men and women should do? Read the following statements. If the statement describes what you think men should do, write *M* on the line. If it describes what you think young women should do, write *W* on the line. Write *M + W* if you think the statement describes what both young men and young women should do.

1. Young _____ should learn to cook and clean.

2. Young _____ should go to college.

3. Young _____ should get some training.

4. Young _____ should get a job.

5. Young unmarried _____ should live with parents or relatives.

6. Young unmarried _____ should live with roommates.

7. Young unmarried _____ should live with their boyfriends or girlfriends.

8. Young _____ should help their parents sometimes.

9. Young _____ should take care of their parents all the time.

10. Young _____ should let their parents support them.

11. Young _____ should take care of themselves.

12. Young _____ should work before they get married.

13. Young _____ should get married and stay home.

14. Young _____ should get married and then work.

15. _____ should get married when they are between 18 and 25 years old.

16. _____ should get married when they are between 26 and 30 years old.

17. _____ should get married when they are over 30 years old.

18. Young married _____ should stay home and take care of the children.

19. Young married _____ should get a job.

20. Young married _____ should get a job and take care of the children.

Look at your answers. Are the things you think men should do different from the things you think women should do? How are they different? Why are they different? Share your answers with your classmates. Give reasons for your choices.

3. DUONG'S PROBLEM

Where are the man and the woman?

How does the man in the picture feel?

Who is the woman on the sofa?

What are they doing?

Are they alone in the house?

Read the story silently. Underline words you don't understand. Your teacher will help you with new words.

A social worker from Child Protective Services came to Duong's house today to talk to him. She said that Duong had broken the law when he beat his daughter, Hoa.

Hoa is 15 years old and an excellent student. Most of the time she is a good daughter, but last week she was not respectful and talked back to her father. This made Duong very angry and he beat her with a stick. Hoa's English teacher saw the bruises and sent her to the nurse's office. The nurse examined Hoa and asked her what happened. Hoa told her about the beating. The nurse called Child Protective Services.

The social worker talked about *child abuse* and told Duong that he had to go to *counseling*. She said that Hoa may have to live with another family if he beats her again. Duong is confused. He doesn't understand. How can Child Protective Services do this? This is his own daughter. He wants her to grow up to be a good person. A good father in his country disciplines his children if they don't obey him. Duong doesn't understand the laws in the United States.

A. COMPREHENSION CHECK.

Listen to your teacher read the sentences and answer yes, no or maybe.

1. The police came to Duong's house today.
2. Duong has a little daughter in elementary school.
3. Hoa is an excellent student.
4. Hoa always listens to her father.
5. Sometimes Duong beats his daughter with a stick.
6. Hoa asked a social worker for help.
7. The school nurse examined Hoa.
8. Hoa cannot live with her father anymore.
9. Duong has to talk to a counselor.
10. Duong understands the American laws.

B. WHAT'S HAPPENING?

First answer the questions orally. Then write down the answers.

1. Who came to Duong's house today?

   _____

2. Why did she come to Duong's house?

   _____

3. Why was Duong angry with his daughter?

   _____

4. What kind of a girl is Hoa? Describe her.

   _____

5. Why did Hoa go to the nurse's office?

   _____

6. What did the nurse ask Hoa?

   _____

7. Who called Child Protective Services?

   _____

8. What may happen if Duong beats his daughter Hoa again?

_____

9. What does Duong have to do so that Hoa can stay in his house?

_____

10. How do fathers discipline their children in Duong's country?

_____

11. Are the laws in the United States the same as in Duong's country?

_____

C. TALK IT OVER.

Discuss the questions with your teacher and classmates. Talk about your personal experiences. Compare your country and the United States. What is the same? What is different?

1. Who disciplined you when you were a child? Your father, your mother or both of them? How did they discipline you?

2. Do you have children? Do they always listen to you? What do you do when your children don't obey you? How do you discipline your children?

3. How can you discipline children without beating them?

4. Are all parents good people? Are there some bad parents in your neighborhood? What do they do?

5. What can happen when adults beat children too hard? Have you ever read a story about this in the newspaper or seen this on TV?

6. Have you ever met a social worker? Did the social worker speak your language or know something about your country and its customs? What can you do if a social worker comes to your house and you don't understand what is happening?

7. What do social workers do? Is it an easy or difficult job? Would you like to be a social worker? Why? Why not?

8. If you knew that someone was abusing a child, what could you do?

9. What is the number of Child Protective Services in your city? Look up the number in the telephone book or call directory assistance and get the number. Write the number below.

   Child Protective Services _____

   Child Abuse Hotline _____

10. What do people in your country do if they have a problem? Do you have counselors and social workers in your country? Who helps children in your country when adults hurt them?

11. Where would you get help if you had a problem? Would you go to a counselor? Why? Why not?

D. WHAT'S THE PROBLEM?

Tell your teacher all the problems in the story. Your teacher will list the problems on the chalkboard.

With your classmates, choose one problem you want to discuss today. Write down the problem.

_____

_____

Find some solutions to this problem. Talk about the consequences of each solution.

What can be done about the problem? Write down some possible solutions.	What might happen if you do that? Write down a possible consequence of each solution.
1. _____ _____	1. _____ _____
2. _____ _____	2. _____ _____
3. _____ _____	3. _____ _____

In small groups, discuss the solutions and consequences. Choose the one solution you think is best. Each group should share its solution with the class. Tell your teacher and classmates why you think this is the best solution. Can your class agree on one solution?

E. WHAT WOULD YOU DO?

Help Duong. You are his friend. Give him some advice. Tell Duong what to do. Write down what you would say to him.

Duong, I think you should _____

_____

_____

F. SPEAK UP!

Work in a small group or with a partner. Choose someone that Duong should talk to. Should he talk to his daughter, a social worker, a friend, a relative, a counselor or somebody else? What should he say? Write a conversation that might help Duong.

Duong: _____

_____ : _____

Duong: _____

_____ : _____

Duong: _____

_____ : _____

G. SHARE YOUR IDEAS.

Write down some things that make parents angry with their children.

1. The children don't study hard in school.

2. They talk back and are not respectful.

3. They don't obey their parents.

4. They are messy.

5. They waste money.

6. _____

7. _____

8. _____

9. _____

10. _____

Put a check (✔) next to the things that make you very angry. Share your list with your classmates. Tell them why these things make you angry. Talk about possible solutions to these problems.

Example: My children don't study very hard in school. This makes me angry, because I want them to go to college. What should I do?

4. VAN AND SONG'S PROBLEM

What is the woman doing?

How does she feel?

Who is next to the woman?

What are the children doing?

How do they feel?

Read the dialogue silently. Underline words you don't understand. Your teacher will help you with new words.

Van: What's the matter Song? Are you sick?

Song: No, I'm not sick. But I'm afraid. Look at the children. I don't know them anymore.

Van: What happened?

Song: Oh, the same old thing. They talk like Americans, look like Americans and dress like Americans. The children don't listen to me. They pretend they don't understand me. They only like American food. When I ask them to help in the house, they say they're too busy.

Van: I'll talk to the children. They must listen to you. You are their mother. They must help you.

Song: Minh says she will move out when she finishes high school next year. She wants to move into her own apartment.

Van: No she won't. She will live here until she marries!

Song: There's nothing you can do. Van, what will happen to us when they all move out and we are old and can't work anymore?

A. COMPREHENSION CHECK.

Listen to the sentences and answer yes, no or maybe.

1. Song is crying.
2. Song is sick.
3. The children like Vietnamese food.
4. The children dress like Americans.
5. The children always listen to their mother.
6. The children help their mother around the house.
7. The children like to go to school.
8. Van says he will talk to the children.
9. Minh wants to move out now.
10. Song is worried about getting old.

B. WHAT'S HAPPENING?

First answer the questions orally. Then write down the answers.

1. Where are Van and Song talking?

_____

2. Where are the children?

_____

3. How do the children like to dress?

_____

4. What language do the children like to speak?

_____

5. What kind of food do the children like?

_____

6. What do the children do when Song talks to them?

_____

7. Who is Minh?

_____

8. When does Minh want to move out?

_____

9. Where does Minh want to move?

_____

10. How long does Van want Minh to live at home?

_____

11. Does Song think her husband can stop the children from moving out?

_____

12. Why is Song afraid?

_____

C. TALK IT OVER.

Discuss the questions with your teacher and classmates. Talk about your personal experiences. Compare your country and the United States. What is the same? What is different?

1. Do you have children? If yes, where do they live? How old are they? Are they married?

2. Do children in your country help parents with work around the house? Do children in the United States help around the house?

3. Are children in the United States more or less independent than in your country?

4. What language do your children or the children of your friends speak at home?

5. Where do most young people in your country live before they get married? Where do most young people in the United States live before they get married?

6. Where did you live after you got married? Where do most people in your country live after they get married? Where do most people in the United States live after they get married?

7. Where do your parents live? How do you help your parents?

8. How do senior citizens in your country pay for food, rent and medical bills? Who takes care of them when they are old and sick?

9. How do older Americans who can't work anymore pay for food, rent and medical bills? Where do they live? Who takes care of them when they are sick?

10. When do most people in your country stop working and retire? In the United States?

11. What kind of work can people in your country who are over 55 years old do? In the United States?

12. Are you afraid of getting old? What do you worry about?

13. Where is life better for senior citizens: in the United States or in your country? How is it better? How is it worse?

14. What can Van and Song do if their children don't help support them when they are older and retired?

D. WHAT'S THE PROBLEM?

Tell your teacher all the problems in the story. Your teacher will list the problems on the chalkboard.

With your classmates, choose one problem you want to discuss today. Write down the problem.

_____

_____

Find some solutions to this problem. Talk about the consequences of each solution.

What can be done about the problem? Write down some possible solutions.

1. _____

_____

2. _____

_____

3. _____

_____

What might happen if you do that? Write down a possible consequence of each solution.

1. _____

_____

2. _____

_____

3. _____

_____

In small groups, discuss the solutions and consequences. Choose the one solution you think is best. Each group should share its solution with the class. Tell your teacher and classmates why you think this is the best solution. Can your class agree on one solution?

E. WHAT WOULD YOU DO?

Help Van and Song. You are their friend. Give them some advice. Tell Van and Song what to do. Write down what you would say to them.

Van and Song, I think you should _____

_____

F. SPEAK UP!

Work in a small group or with a partner. Choose someone that Van and Song should talk to. Should they talk to their children, a relative or somebody else? What should they say? Write a conversation that might help Van and Song.

_____ : _____

_____ : _____

_____ : _____

_____ : _____

_____ : _____

_____ : _____

G. SHARE YOUR IDEAS.

Think about growing older. Write down what you want to do when you are older and how you can prepare yourself.

1. What city do you want to live in? _____

2. Who do you want to live with? _____

3. Do you want to live in a house, or apartment, or a home for

   senior citizens or somewhere else? _____

4. Do you want to travel? If yes, where? _____

5. How do you want to save money? _____

6. Who will pay for food, medical bills and rent? _____

7. How will you take good care of your health? _____

8. If you get sick, who do you want to take care of you? _____

Share your answers with your classmates. Do you have the same ideas about growing older?

MORE PROBLEMS

RAUL'S PROBLEM

Raul Herrera is a third-grade student at Morrison Elementary School. He works hard in school. He likes his teacher and most of the students in his class, but there are some big boys who pick on him. They take his lunch money, spit on him and tell him to go back to Mexico. Yesterday they pushed him in the mud and tore his new jacket.

Raul's mother wants to put him into another school where there are more students from Mexico, but Raul likes his school and his teacher and does not want to change schools. What should Raul and his mother do?

LANI'S PROBLEM

Lani is going to have to stay home again this week. She has a black eye, a swollen lip, bruises on her arms and one of her front teeth is loose. She doesn't want her friends to see her. She is ashamed to go out. Her husband beat her again.

Lani's husband says that he is sorry and that he will never do this again, but he always says this after he beats her. Lani wants to leave him, but she does not want to leave her four children. She has never had a job and she feels that she can't support the children without her husband's help.

What should she do? Can anybody help her?

TONY AND ANTONIO'S PROBLEM

Tony is in his last year of high school. Tony is not happy about graduating from high school because he will have to go to work full time in his father Antonio's garage. He hates fixing cars and he does not want to spend the rest of his life doing that. He loves music and he wants to be a classical guitarist. His father Antonio gets angry when he talks about becoming a musician.

Antonio can't wait until his son Tony graduates and comes to work full time in the garage. Then Antonio can have more free time and relax a little. He is not young anymore. He is tired of working 60 hours a week. He wants a vacation. He wants to go back to his native country to visit his family. He is looking forward to the day when Tony will take over the shop and he can retire.

Now both Tony and Antonio are worried about their futures. What can they do?

THE HUYNH'S PROBLEM

Six weeks ago Mrs. Huynh's mother-in-law came from Vietnam to live with the Huynh family. They had not seen her since 1975 and she had never met her grandson and two granddaughters. Everyone had looked forward to her arrival. It would be nice to have her here. She could look after the children while the parents worked, and she could cook for the family.

Now six weeks after her arrival, the granddaughters are hurt and angry. They say that their grandmother doesn't like them. She spoils their brother and makes them do all the work. They are the maids and he is the "Emperor of China". Grandma even gives him better food. He gets meat and rice, and they only get to eat the soup the meat was cooked in and some vegetables. The girls feel that this is not fair. They complain to their mother but they are afraid to say anything to their father.

What's happening here? Can you help the Huynhs solve their problem?

ROBERTA'S PROBLEM

Roberta's mother, who is 75 years old, just moved in with Roberta and her husband. Roberta is a teacher and works every morning. Her husband is a salesman and is gone a lot.

Roberta gets along well with her mother, but there is something that worries her. Her mother is very forgetful. She forgets to turn off the gas stove. She leaves the house unlocked when she goes out and she forgets many other important things.

Roberta is afraid to go to work and leave her alone. What's wrong? What can Roberta do?

1. DOLORES' PROBLEM

Where are the children and the woman?

Are they all her children?

What are the children doing?

How does the woman in the picture feel?

Read the story silently. Underline words you don't understand. Your teacher will help you with new words.

Dolores and her three children live in a rented house next to an apartment building. They have a big backyard.

Some children from the apartments next door come to play in Dolores' yard. There is no playground or park nearby, and Dolores has a swingset. Many of the children's mothers work and do not come home until six o'clock. Some of the children are home alone.

At first, having the children was not a problem, but now there are often six children in Dolores' yard. Sometimes the children are noisy and fight. The neighbors complain about the noise. Dolores' landlord is angry because the children break things. Dolores' husband is upset. He doesn't want any trouble with the neighbors and the landlord.

A. COMPREHENSION CHECK.

Listen to your teacher read the sentences and answer yes, no or maybe.

1. Dolores is married.
2. She lives in an apartment.
3. Dolores bought a house last year.
4. Her children like to play in the yard.
5. All the children in the neighborhood live in houses with yards.
6. Many children play in Dolores' yard.
7. The children never fight.
8. Dolores gets money for baby-sitting.
9. Dolores' landlord is angry.
10. Dolores' neighbors like to watch children play.

B. WHAT'S HAPPENING?

First answer the questions orally. Then write down the answers.

1. Where does Dolores live?

_____

2. What does Dolores have in her yard?

_____

3. How many children does she have?

_____

4. Where is the apartment building?

_____

5. Does the apartment building have a place where children can play?

_____

6. Where do the children like to go after school?

_____

7. Is that OK with Dolores? Why? Why not?

_____

8. Why is Dolores' landlord angry?

_____

9. Why are the neighbors angry?

_____

10. Why don't the children play at their own homes?

_____

C. TALK IT OVER.

Discuss the questions with your teacher and classmates. Talk about your personal experiences. Compare your country and the United States. What is the same? What is different?

1. Why do so many mothers in the United States work?

2. Who takes care of their children while they work?

3. Do most mothers in your country stay home or do they have jobs?

4. Who takes care of the children in your country when parents are busy?

5. Do most families live in a house or in an apartment in your country?

6. Do you live in a house or in an apartment now?

7. If you have children, where do they play? What do they do after school?

8. Where do your neighbors' children play? Are there parks and playgrounds nearby?

9. Why shouldn't you leave young children home alone? What could happen?

10. Should young children go to parks alone? What could happen?

11. What should working parents do if they can't be home when their children come home from school?

12. Where can you find a good baby-sitter for your children if you have to work?

13. What important information and telephone numbers should you give your babysitter?

D. WHAT'S THE PROBLEM?

Tell your teacher all the problems in the story. Your teacher will list the problems on the chalkboard.

With your classmates, choose one problem you want to discuss today. Write down the problem.

_____

_____

Find some solutions to this problem. Talk about the consequences of each solution.

What can be done about the problem? Write down some possible solutions.

1. _____

   _____

2. _____

   _____

3. _____

   _____

What might happen if you do that? Write down a possible consequence of each solution.

1. _____

   _____

2. _____

   _____

3. _____

   _____

In small groups, discuss the solutions and consequences. Choose the one solution you think is best. Each group should share its solution with the class. Tell your teacher and classmates why you think this is the best solution. Can your class agree on one solution?

E. WHAT WOULD YOU DO?

Help Dolores. You are her friend. Give her some advice. Tell Dolores what to do. Write down what you would say to her.

Dolores, I think you should _____

_____

_____

SPEAK UP!   Work in a small group or with a partner. Choose exercise 1 or 2.

1. Choose someone that Dolores should talk to. Should she talk to the landlord, the children, their parents, the angry neighbors or somebody else? What should she say? Write a conversation that might help Dolores.

Dolores: _____

_____ : _____

Dolores: _____

_____ : _____

Dolores: _____

_____ : _____

2. Choose someone that Dolores should write to. Should she write to the landlord, the children's parents, the angry neighbors or somebody else? What should she write? Write a letter that might help Dolores.

Dear _____

_____

_____

_____

_____

_____

_____

_____

_____

G. SHARE YOUR IDEAS.

Your seven-year-old son comes home from school at two o'clock. You get off work at four o'clock. You need a baby-sitter. What's most important to you? Circle what you think is important. Add your own ideas to the list.

My baby-sitter should . . .

come to my house	have a yard	not charge too much money
live near my house	have a safe house	be clean
be a relative	know what to do in an emergency	be strict
be from my country	have a car	be patient
speak my language	pick up my child at school	_____
speak good English	have other children of her own	
help my child with homework	watch not more than five children	_____
have a day-care license	ask parents to keep sick children at home	_____

Share your answers with your classmates. Tell them why some things are very important to you and why other things are not very important to you.

2. YONAS' PROBLEM

What are these two men doing?

Are they friends?

What is the man looking at in his apartment?

How do each of the two men feel?

Read the dialogue silently. Underline words you don't understand. Your teacher will help you with new words.

Yonas:	This is Yonas in apartment 13 on the second floor. Remember, I called twice last week about the leaking roof? Now the plaster is falling from the ceiling. I'm worried about my children. They sleep in this room.
Mr. Kingsley:	What did you do to the ceiling? It was OK when you moved in last month.
Yonas:	We didn't do anything. It rained a lot and the roof is bad.
Mr. Kingsley:	The ceiling was OK last month when we painted your place.
Yonas:	It rained after that. Come and take a look at the roof and ceiling. Then you can see for yourself that the the roof is bad.
Mr. Kingsley:	I'm busy this week. I don't know what you people expect. The rent is cheap. If I have to put on a new roof, I have to raise your rent.
Yonas:	I can't afford to pay more rent. Maybe you can patch the roof. This apartment isn't safe. The ceiling may fall down any day!

A. COMPREHENSION CHECK.

Listen to your teacher read
the sentences and answer
yes, no or maybe.

1. Yonas has children.
2. Yonas is talking to the landlord.
3. This is the first time Yonas called the landlord.
4. Yonas is worried about a leaking toilet.
5. Yonas has been living here for two years.
6. The landlord is going to fix the ceiling this week.
7. Yonas sleeps in the room with the bad ceiling.
8. The landlord thinks Yonas did something to the ceiling.
9. The landlord and Yonas are good friends.
10. The landlord will raise the rent.

B. WHAT'S HAPPENING?

First answer the questions
orally. Then write down the
answers.

1. Which apartment does Yonas live in?

   _____

2. When did Yonas move in?

   _____

3. How many times did Yonas call the landlord last week?

   _____

4. What's wrong with the roof?

   _____

5. What's wrong with the ceiling?

   _____

6. Who sleeps in the room with the bad ceiling?

   _____

7. How was the ceiling last month?

   _____

(*Continued on next page.*)

8. Why is the ceiling bad now?

_____

9. Why is Yonas worried?

_____

10. What will happen if the landlord puts on a new roof?

_____

11. Why can't Yonas pay more rent?

_____

12. What else can the landlord do to the roof?

_____

C. TALK IT OVER.

Discuss the questions with your teacher and classmates. Talk about your personal experiences. Compare your country and the United States. What is the same? What is different?

1. Do most people rent or own houses in your country? Did you rent or own your house?

2. How do you find good housing in your country? Is it easier to find good housing in your country or in the United States?

3. Who fixes broken things in your home in your country? Who fixes broken things in your home in the United States?

4. What kinds of problems do you have in your home?

5. If you rent, who talks to the landlord when you have a problem? Do you have a good or bad landlord? Why?

6. If you rent, do you communicate with the landlord by phone, mail or in person?

7. If you rent, how long do you have to wait for the landlord to make repairs? Does he or she always fix everything?

8. What can you do if your landlord won't fix things?

9. Do you have laws in your country that can protect the tenant? Do you know about the laws that protect the tenant in the United States? Is there an agency that can help you if you have problems with your landlord? Find the name and phone number of the agency and write them here:

_____

10. Do you have laws in your country that can protect the landlord? Do you know about the laws that protect the landlord in the United States?

D. WHAT'S THE PROBLEM?

Tell your teacher all the problems in the story. Your teacher will list the problems on the chalkboard.

With your classmates, choose one problem you want to discuss today. Write down the problem.

_____

_____

Find some solutions to this problem. Talk about the consequences of each solution.

What can be done about the problem? Write down some possible solutions.

1. _____

_____

2. _____

_____

3. _____

_____

What might happen if you do that? Write down a possible consequence of each solution.

1. _____

_____

2. _____

_____

3. _____

_____

In small groups, discuss the solutions and consequences. Choose the one solution you think is best. Each group should share its solution with the class. Tell your teacher and classmates why you think this is the best solution. Can your class agree on one solution?

E. WHAT WOULD YOU DO?

Help Yonas. You are his friend. Give him some advice. Tell Yonas what to do. Write down what you would say to him.

Yonas, I think you should _____

_____

_____

F. SPEAK UP!

Work in a small group or with a partner. Choose someone that Yonas should talk to. Should he talk to a friend, a lawyer, a tenant's assistance center or somebody else? What should he say? Write a conversation that might help Yonas.

Yonas: _____

_____ : _____

Yonas: _____

_____ : _____

Yonas: _____

_____ : _____

G. SHARE YOUR IDEAS.

1. Sometimes the landlord must pay to fix a problem. Sometimes a tenant should pay to fix a problem. Check who should fix each problem.

	Tenant	Landlord
1. The roof is leaking.		
2. A lightbulb is burned out.		
3. Your TV is broken.		
4. The stove is leaking gas.		
5. A window is broken. You don't know who broke it.		
6. A window is broken. Your son broke the window.		
7. The smoke detector is broken.		
8. Diapers clogged the toilet.		
9. A big pan was dropped in the sink. Now the sink is cracked.		
10. The refrigerator is broken.		
11. A cigarette burned the carpet.		
12. The carpet is old and worn out.		
13. There are bugs in the apartment.		
14. The toilet is leaking.		
15. The lock on the front door is broken.		

Share your answers with your classmates. Does everyone have the same answers?

2. What's wrong in your house or apartment? Write a letter to your landlord to ask for repairs. First tell the teacher what's wrong in your house or apartment. Your teacher will make a list and write it on the board. Then you and your teacher can write a letter to the landlord on the board. Copy the letter and send it to the landlord when you have a problem.

3. THE MONTOYAS' PROBLEM

What is the woman doing?

What is the man outside doing?

How does the woman feel?

Who do you think the woman is talking to?

Read the story silently. Underline words you don't understand. Your teacher will help you with new words.

Bertha Montoya, her husband and three children live in a dangerous part of town. They are afraid to go out at night because there are so many robberies and other crimes in their neighborhood. They don't have enough money to move to a safer neighborhood.

From her kitchen window, Bertha can see the people and cars that come and go. Last Saturday night Bertha saw a man selling something in the alley behind her apartment. Her teenage son told her that the man was selling drugs. Bertha's husband was at work. Bertha called the police, but they didn't come for a long time, and the people in the alley were gone when the police arrived.

When Bertha's husband came home and heard that she had called the police, he was angry. He told her that this was not their business and she should never call the police again.

A. COMPREHENSION CHECK.

Listen to your teacher read the sentences and answer yes, no or maybe.

1. Bertha has three children.
2. Bertha lives near a pharmacy.
3. Bertha's children go to high school.
4. Bertha's neighborhood is safe.
5. There is a lot of crime in Bertha's neighborhood.
6. A man was selling a TV in the alley.
7. Bertha's husband worked on Saturday night.
8. Bertha called the police.
9. The police came immediately.
10. Bertha's husband was angry that she called the police.

B. WHAT'S HAPPENING?

First answer the questions orally. Then write down the answers.

1. Where does Bertha Montoya live?

   _____

2. Why are the Montoyas afraid to go out at night?

   _____

3. Can the Montoyas move to a better neighborhood? Why? Why not?

   _____

4. What did Bertha see last Saturday night?

   _____

5. Who told Bertha what the man was selling?

   _____

6. Where was Bertha's husband Saturday night?

   _____

7. What did Bertha do?

   _____

8. When did the police come?

_____

9. Why didn't the police arrest the drug dealers?

_____

10. Why was Bertha's husband angry?

_____

11. Does Bertha's husband want her to call the police next time? Why? Why not?

_____

C. TALK IT OVER.

Discuss the questions with your teacher and classmates. Talk about your personal experiences. Compare your country and the United States. What is the same? What is different?

1. What are drugs?

2. Is it legal to buy and sell drugs in the United States? In your country?

3. Where do drugs come from?

4. Is it easy or difficult to buy drugs? Are they cheap or expensive?

5. Do young people or old people use drugs more? Are you worried that your children might use drugs?

6. Why do people use drugs?

7. Why do people sell drugs?

8. What can happen to people who use drugs?

9. Where can people with a drug problem get help?

10. If you saw someone selling drugs would you call the police?

11. Did you ever call the police in your country? If not, why not?

12. Have you or a friend ever called the police in the United States? When? Why?

13. Did the police come right away? What did they do?

14. What kind of crime is in your neighborhood in the United States?

15. What kind of crime was in your neighborhood in your country?

16. Do you feel safer in the United States or in your country? Why?

17. Do you think you can do something to stop drug dealers, robberies and crime in your neighborhood? What can you do?

D. WHAT'S THE PROBLEM?

Tell your teacher all the problems in the story. Your teacher will list the problems on the chalkboard.

With your classmates, choose one problem you want to discuss today. Write down the problem.

_____

_____

Find some solutions to this problem. Talk about the consequences of each solution.

What can be done about the problem? Write down some possible solutions.

1. _____

   _____

2. _____

   _____

3. _____

   _____

What might happen if you do that? Write down a possible consequence of each solution.

1. _____

   _____

2. _____

   _____

3. _____

   _____

In small groups, discuss the solutions and consequences. Choose the one solution you think is best. Each group should share its solution with the class. Tell your teacher and classmates why you think this is the best solution. Can your class agree on one solution?

E. WHAT WOULD YOU DO?

Help the Montoyas. You are their friend. Give them some advice. Tell the Montoyas what to do. Write down what you would say to them.

I think you should _____

_____

F. SPEAK UP!

Work in a small group or with a partner. Choose someone that the Montoyas should talk to. Should they talk to the police, the neighbors, each other or somebody else? What should they say? Write a conversation that might help the Montoyas.

_____ : _____

_____ : _____

_____ : _____

_____ : _____

_____ : _____

_____ : _____

G. SHARE YOUR IDEAS.

You are going to move to a new neighborhood. What is important to you? What is not important to you?

Look at the list below and put a check (✓) next to what is important and what is not important. Add your own ideas to the list.

	Important	Not Important
1. The neighborhood has to be clean.		
2. The neighbors have to be friendly.		
3. There have to be stores nearby.		
4. I have to live near work.		
5. I have to live near the highway.		
6. I have to live near schools.		
7. I have to live near a park.		
8. I have to pay low rent.		
9. I have to live in a safe neighborhood.		
10. I have to live near relatives.		
11. I have to live near the beach.		
12. I have to live near the bus.		
13. I have to live near a laundromat.		
14. I have to live in a quiet part of town.		
15. I have to live near people from my country.		

_____

_____

Share your answers with your classmates. Tell them why some things are important to you and why other things are not very important to you.

MORE PROBLEMS

LU'S PROBLEM

Lu is a widow with four young children. She just came to the United States from Thailand, where she lived in a refugee camp with her father-in-law and mother-in-law. She is happy to be in the United States with her brother Seng and his family. He and his wife and their three children live in a two-bedroom apartment. Lu has been staying with them.

Yesterday Seng's landlord told him that Lu and her children had to move out. He did not want to have 10 people in a two-bedroom apartment. Lu is afraid to live alone with her children. She has always lived with relatives. She doesn't speak English, she can't read and she can't drive.

Seng tried to find a larger house or apartment to rent, but nobody wants to rent to a family with seven children. What can they do?

HAILU'S PROBLEM

Hailu and his family rented a nice house last week. They are the first Ethiopian people in the area. The rent is cheap, the house is large and there are stores and schools nearby. Hailu and his family were happy that they moved to such a nice and safe neighborhood.

Unfortunately the neighbors are not very friendly. They do not like Hailu and his family. Last week some teenagers drove by and threw eggs at Hailu's house. This week trash was dumped on his front yard. Yesterday some children kicked his son, called him bad names and told him to go back where he came from. Hailu doesn't know what to do. He has signed a one-year lease. He doesn't want to move again. Why don't these people like him and his family? Who can help them?

PETRA'S PROBLEM

Petra and her family share a large house with another family because they do not have enough money to rent their own house. At first everything was fine, but for the last few months Petra has been very angry and unhappy.

The family that shares the house with them is nice, but they don't help with the cleaning. Petra and her daughter have to do all the cleaning. The other family does not care if the house is dirty or messy. Petra thinks that this is not fair. What can she do?

ROSA'S PROBLEM

Two months ago three young men moved next door to Rosa and her children. The men stay up late, play loud music and have lots of parties. The walls of the building are thin, and Rosa and her children can't sleep because their neighbors make so much noise. She is afraid to knock on their door and complain to them because they drink a lot and are not very polite.

Rosa called the landlord, but he didn't do anything. Rosa is very unhappy. She is always tired when she wakes up in the morning. She doesn't want to move, because the apartment is near her children's school, near the bus stop and near her job. What can she do?

AMANUEL'S PROBLEM

Amanuel and his wife found a sunny apartment near the bus stop. The rent is not expensive, but the apartment is not in very good shape. The walls are dirty, the mirror in the bathroom is cracked, the carpet has some stains on it and there is a hole in the kitchen floor.

The landlord asked for a $300 security and cleaning deposit. Amanuel expected him to paint the walls, replace the mirror and fix the kitchen floor, but the landlord has not wanted to do this. Now Amanuel is worried that when they move out in one or two years, the landlord will charge him for the damaged things. What can Amanuel do?

THE RAMIREZ' PROBLEM

Elario and Sara's dream came true when they bought the little three-bedroom house near the taco shop where they both work. The house was not expensive, because it is not in the best part of town and it need lots of repairs. Elario and Sara work hard to make the monthly mortgage payments. The house is perfect for them and their two teenage children.

Unfortunately, in the past year there have been many gang fights in their neighborhood. Every month someone gets hurt. By the time the police come, the gang members are gone.

Some of the teenagers in the neighborhood belong to these gangs. Elario's 13-year-old son thinks the gang members are great because they have money and cool cars, and because they "talk big." Elario and Sara are also worried about their 15-year-old daughter Ramona. She is very pretty and many of the neighborhood boys are interested in her. What can Elario and Sara do to keep their children safe and out of gangs?

1. LUIGI AND PAULA'S PROBLEM

Where is the man?

What is he doing?

How does he feel?

Who is coming towards the house?

How does she feel?

Read the story silently. Underline words you don't understand. Your teacher will help you with new words.

Luigi is waiting for his wife Paula to come home. He is very angry. Paula went shopping again. She probably took the credit cards and charged some more things. He just got a bill for the things she charged last month. It was a large bill. He doesn't know if he can pay it.

Every month Luigi writes checks for the house payment, car payment, furniture payments and the payments on their three credit cards. He worries that there will not be enough money for all the bills, food, insurance and other expenses this month. They don't have that much money in their savings account. What will they do if he loses his job? How will he pay all the bills?

Luigi loves Paula. He wants her to have nice things, but he knows he can't pay for all the things she wants. Paula must stop charging things until the bills are paid off. Paula doesn't understand. She thinks that with these credit cards they can buy anything they want and then pay later. She thinks Luigi worries too much.

A. COMPREHENSION CHECK.

Listen to your teacher read
the sentences and answer
yes, no or maybe.

1. Paula is waiting for her husband to come home.
2. Luigi is angry.
3. Paula is at work.
4. Paula likes to go shopping.
5. Paula pays cash for everything.
6. Luigi and Paula have to pay many bills every month.
7. Paula spent a lot of money last month.
8. Luigi lost his job.
9. Luigi has lots of money in a savings account.
10. Luigi wants Paula to stop charging things.

B. WHAT'S HAPPENING?

First answer the questions
orally. Then write down the
answers.

1. What is Luigi doing?

   _____

2. Where is Paula?

   _____

3. How does Paula pay for the things she buys?

   _____

4. Why is Luigi angry?

   _____

5. What kind of payments do Luigi and Paula have every month?

   _____

6. How many credit cards do they have?

   _____

7. What is Luigi worried about?

   _____

(Continued on next page.)

8. How does Luigi feel about Paula?

_____

9. What does Paula think she can do with the credit cards?

_____

10. What might happen if Luigi loses his job?

_____

C. TALK IT OVER.

Discuss the questions with your teacher and classmates. Talk about your personal experiences. Compare your country and the United States. What is the same? What is different?

1. Who does the shopping in your family? Where do you go shopping? What do you like to buy?

2. Do you use credit cards or do you pay cash for the things you buy? Have you bought anything on credit? What?

3. How do people in your country pay for the things they buy? Do they pay cash, write a check or use credit cards? What about in the United States?

4. Can you go shopping in your country if you don't have any money? Can you go shopping in the United States if you don't have any money? If yes, how?

5. Who can get a credit card? Is it easy or difficult to get a credit card?

6. If you have a credit card and you charge something this month, when do you have to pay for it? What happens if you only pay part of the bill?

7. Is it good to have a credit card sometimes? If so, when? Why?

8. How can using credit cards get people in trouble? What can happen?

9. What is a bad credit rating? Who gets a bad credit rating? Is a good credit rating important? Why?

10. Would you like to have a credit card? Do you want your wife, husband or children to have credit cards? Why? Why not?

11. Many people buy cars and furniture on credit. What happens if they can't make the payments?

12. What should you do if you lose a credit card?

13. Do you think it is better to pay cash for the things you buy or buy them on credit? Why?

14. Do you agree with Paula or Luigi in this story? Why?

D. WHAT'S THE PROBLEM?

Tell your teacher all the problems in the story. Your teacher will list the problems on the chalkboard.

With your classmates, choose one problem you want to discuss today. Write down the problem.

_____

_____

Find some solutions to this problem. Talk about the consequences of each solution.

What can be done about the problem? Write down some possible solutions.

1. _____

    _____

2. _____

    _____

3. _____

    _____

What might happen if you do that? Write down a possible consequence of each solution.

1. _____

    _____

2. _____

    _____

3. _____

    _____

In small groups, discuss the solutions and consequences. Choose the one solution you think is best. Each group should share its solution with the class. Tell your teacher and classmates why you think this is the best solution. Can your class agree on one solution?

E. WHAT WOULD YOU DO?

Help Luigi and Paula. You are their friend. Give them some advice. Tell Luigi and Paula what to do. Write down what you would say to them. Would you talk to both of them or to just one of them? Who would you talk to?

_____ , I think you should _____
(name)

_____

F. SPEAK UP!

Work in a small group or with a partner. Write a conversation between Luigi and Paula. What should they say? How can they solve their problems without making each other angry?

_____ : _____

_____ : _____

_____ : _____

_____ : _____

_____ : _____

_____ : _____

G. SHARE YOUR IDEAS.

You don't have much money in the bank, but you have a good job. You can use a credit card or get a loan for the things you want to buy. Look at the list. Make some careful choices. Underline the things you would buy on credit. Circle the things you would pay for with cash. Cross out the things you would not buy now. Add your own ideas to the list.

new clothes	a new car	a used car
a watch	a diamond ring	a TV
furniture	a house	a computer
a VCR	a stove	a refrigerator
a washer	a dryer	a motorcycle
_____	_____	_____

Share your list with your classmates. Give reasons for your choices. Ask them what they think.

Example: I would buy a washer on credit because going to the laundromat is expensive, and I could save money by doing the wash at home.

2. KHANH'S PROBLEM

Where are the men?

What are they doing?

How does the older man feel?

How does the younger man feel?

Read the dialogue silently. Underline words you don't understand. Your teacher will help you with new words.

Khanh and his father Phat live in an apartment. Khanh does most of the shopping, cooking and cleaning because Phat is sick and old. Khanh is an assistant manager in a supermarket.

Phat: Where are you going?

Khanh: I'm going to the bank to put our money in a savings account.

Phat: The bank? A savings account? You can't do that! Banks are not safe. I lost all my money in a bank in Vietnam.

Khanh: But father, this is not Vietnam. This is the United States. The banks are different here. Our money is safer in the banks than in the house.

Phat: We should take the money and buy gold. Gold is better than money. We can hide it here under the floor.

Khanh: Father, it's not safe to keep money or gold around the house. Every week someone we know gets robbed. I don't want to have to worry about it.

A. COMPREHENSION CHECK.

Listen to your teacher read
the sentences and answer
yes, no or maybe.

1. Khanh and Phat live in an apartment.
2. Phat works.
3. Khanh works full time.
4. Khanh is going to the supermarket.
5. Phat likes banks.
6. Phat comes from Vietnam.
7. Phat wants to buy gold.
8. Khanh also wants to buy gold.
9. Many of Khanh's friends and neighbors get robbed.
10. Phat lost all his money in a bank in Vietnam.
11. Khanh thinks banks in the United States are safe.

B. WHAT'S HAPPENING?

First answer the questions
orally. Then write down the
answers.

1. Where does Khanh work?

   _____

2. Does Phat work?

   _____

3. Who takes care of Phat?

   _____

4. Where is Khanh going?

   _____

5. What does Khanh want to do at the bank?

   _____

6. Does Phat think banks are safe?

   _____

7. What happened to Phat's money in Vietnam?

   _____

8. What does Phat want to buy?

_____

9. Where does Phat want to hide the gold?

_____

10. Why is Khanh worried about keeping money or gold at home?

_____

11. Where does Khanh think the money would be safe?

_____

C. TALK IT OVER.

Discuss the questions with your teacher and classmates. Talk about your personal experiences. Compare your country and the United States. What is the same? What is different?

1. Do you go to a bank sometimes? If yes, what do you do at the bank?

2. When are the banks in your neighborhood open? What days are they closed?

3. Do you have any savings? If yes, are you saving your money for something special? What?

4. Did you have any savings in your country? Where did you keep your savings? Why?

5. Do people in your country save money, gold or jewelry? Why?

6. Are the banks in your country safe? Did you ever lose any money in a bank? If yes, what happened?

7. Are banks in the United States safer than in other countries? If yes, why?

8. What does _FDIC insured_ mean? Who insures money in U.S. banks?

9. What is a safe-deposit box? What do some people put in it? Is a safe-deposit box free? If not, how much is it? What would you put in it?

10. Some people put their money in a savings account to get _interest_. What is interest? What interest rates do banks give? How much money do you need to open an account with interest? Can you take your money out anytime?

11. Have any of your relatives, neighbors or friends been robbed? Who? What was stolen?

12. Do you think burglars know who keeps money and jewelry at home and who keeps it in the bank? Whom will burglars rob more often?

13. Is it easy to buy and sell gold and jewelry in your country? In the United States?

14. Do you think Khanh and Phat should buy gold or open a savings account? Why?

WHAT'S THE PROBLEM?

Tell your teacher all the problems in the story. Your teacher will list the problems on the chalkboard.

With your classmates, choose one problem you want to discuss today. Write down the problem.

_____

_____

Find some solutions to this problem. Talk about the consequences of each solution.

What can be done about the problem? Write down some possible solutions.	What might happen if you do that? Write down a possible consequence of each solution.
1. _____	1. _____
2. _____	2. _____
3. _____	3. _____

In small groups, discuss the solutions and consequences. Choose the one solution you think is best. Each group should share its solution with the class. Tell your teacher and classmates why you think this is the best solution. Can your class agree on one solution?

E. WHAT WOULD YOU DO?

Help Khanh. You are his friend. Give him some advice. Tell Khanh what to do. Write down what you would say to him.

Khanh, I think you should _____

_____

_____

F. SPEAK UP!

Work in a small group or with a partner. Choose someone that Khanh should talk to. Should he talk to a friend, a bank teller or somebody else? What should he say? Write a conversation that might help Khanh.

Khanh: _____

_____ : _____

Khanh: _____

_____ : _____

Khanh: _____

_____ : _____

G. SHARE YOUR IDEAS.

Work in groups. Talk with your classmates about how you save money. Then write down the ideas.

I can save money on rent by

1. sharing a house with many people.

2. _____

3. _____

I can save money on food by

1. using coupons when I shop at the market.

2. _____

3. _____

I can save money on clothing by

1. making my own clothes.

2. _____

3. _____

(Continued on next page.)

I can save money on water by

1. taking short showers.

2. _____

3. _____

I can save money on utilities (gas and electricity) by

1. turning down the heat at night.

2. _____

3. _____

I can save money on transportation (car repairs, gas, bus, etc.) by

1. keeping the right air pressure in the tires.

2. _____

3. _____

Other ways to save money:

1. take $5.00 or more out of every paycheck and put the money in a savings account.

2. _____

3. _____

Other ways to make extra money:

1. recycle aluminum cans.

2. _____

3. _____

3. ANGELA'S PROBLEM

What do you see in the picture?

Where are the man and the woman?

What are they doing?

Why are they angry?

Read the story silently. Underline words you don't understand. Your teacher will help you with new words.

Angela and her husband Ivan had a big fight yesterday. Angela was angry because Ivan sent his parents and brothers $500 again. Their savings account is now empty.

Angela and Ivan both have jobs. Ivan is a welder and Angela cleans houses. Their three children attend school. When Angela went to work two years ago, she hoped to save some money to buy new furniture, a new car and maybe even a house.

Now she knows that they will never be able to save any money because Ivan's family always asks for money and Ivan sends it to them. He says that they are his family and if they need money he must help them. He never asks Angela if he can send the money, he just does it. Angela thinks that this is not fair, because Ivan sends the extra money that she earns.

If all the extra money she makes will go to Ivan's family, then Angela does not want to work. She would like to stay home and be a homemaker and mother. None of the women in Ivan's family have jobs. Why should her money go to them? She thinks that Ivan's family is taking advantage of them.

A. COMPREHENSION CHECK.

Listen to your teacher read the sentences and answer yes, no or maybe.

1. Angela and Ivan had a fight.
2. Angela sent some money to her family.
3. Ivan has a job.
4. Angela does not have a job.
5. Angela and Ivan have lots of money in the bank.
6. Ivan's family is poor and needs money.
7. Ivan thinks he must help his family.
8. Angela wants to save money for furniture, a car and a house.
9. Ivan asks Angela if he can send his family money.
10. Angela does not like to work.

B. WHAT'S HAPPENING?

First answer the questions orally. Then write down the answers.

1. What did Angela and Ivan do yesterday?

   _____

2. Why was Angela angry with Ivan?

   _____

3. How much money did Ivan send to his family?

   _____

4. How much money do Ivan and Angela have in the bank now?

   _____

5. What kind of work does Ivan do?

   _____

6. Does Angela have a job? What does she do?

   _____

7. How long has Angela been working?

   _____

8. What does Angela want to do with the extra money they have?

_____

9. Who decides how the extra money will be spent, Angela or Ivan?

_____

10. Why does Angela think this is not fair?

_____

11. What might Angela do if Ivan sends all the extra money to his family?

_____

C. TALK IT OVER.

Discuss the questions with your teacher and classmates. Talk about your personal experiences. Compare your country and the United States. What is the same? What is different?

1. Are you married or single? Do you have a job? Is your spouse (husband or wife) earning money, too?

2. What do you spend your money on every month?

3. Do you have any money left after you pay the bills? If yes, what do you do with the money?

4. Do you think people should save some money every month? If yes, what should they save money for?

5. Do you think married sons and daughters should help their parents and brothers and sisters? Why? Why not?

6. Where is your family? Do they need help? Do you help your family? How?

7. Do both the husband and the wife earn money in your country? Who decides what they should spend their money on?

8. Do married couples in your country fight about money sometimes? What are the fights about? What are the problems?

9. Do you think Ivan is doing the right thing when he sends their savings to his family? Why? Why not?

10. Do you think Angela has a good reason to be angry about the money? Why? Why not?

D. WHAT'S THE PROBLEM?

Tell your teacher all the problems in the story. Your teacher will list the problems on the chalkboard.

With your classmates, choose one problem you want to discuss today. Write down the problem.

_____

_____

Find some solutions to this problem. Talk about the consequences of each solution.

What can be done about the problem? Write down some possible solutions.

1. _____

_____

2. _____

_____

3. _____

_____

What might happen if you do that? Write down a possible consequence of each solution.

1. _____

_____

2. _____

_____

3. _____

_____

In small groups, discuss the solutions and consequences. Choose the one solution you think is best. Each group should share its solution with the class. Tell your teacher and classmates why you think this is the best solution. Can your class agree on one solution?

E. WHAT WOULD YOU DO?

Help Ivan and Angela. They are your friends. Give them some advice. Tell Ivan and Angela what to do. Write down what you would say to them. Would you talk to both of them or to just one of them? Who would you talk to?

_____ , I think you should _____
(name)

_____

_____

F. SPEAK UP!

Work in a small group or with a partner. Write a conversation between Ivan and Angela. What should they say? How can they solve their problems and not make each other angry?

_____ : _____

_____ : _____

_____ : _____

_____ : _____

_____ : _____

_____ : _____

G. SHARE YOUR IDEAS.

Work with a partner or in a small group.

The Ramirez family earns $1480 a month after taxes and other deductions. There are five people in the family. The children are 8, 10 and 14 years old. Both parents work. Mrs. Ramirez is working part time. They have one car that is paid for. How much can they spend on rent, food, utilities and other things every month?

FAMILY BUDGET

Rent	$_____		
Electricity/gas	$_____		
Telephone	$_____		
Clothes	$_____		
Food	$_____		
Car insurance	$_____		
Gasoline	$_____		
_____	$_____	Income:	$1480.00
_____	$_____	Expenses:	_____
Total monthly expenses	$_____	How much is left:	_____

Is there money left over? What should the Ramirez family do with their money?

Share your list with your classmates. Can you make a family budget for your own family?

MORE PROBLEMS

ADAR'S PROBLEM

Adar bought a pair of new shoes at a large department store one month ago. She paid $40 for the shoes. This was a lot of money, but Adar needed good shoes. She had to walk to school every day.

Today while she was walking to school, the sole came off her left shoe. She was very upset. She took the shoes to the repair shop, but the repairman couldn't fix them. Adar doesn't have the money to buy another pair of shoes. What can she do?

VLADIMIR'S PROBLEM

It's Friday. Vladimir just cashed his paycheck. He is standing at the bus stop and is waiting for the bus. A strange man walks up to him and starts talking to him. The man shows Vladimir a beautiful gold bracelet and asks him if he wants to buy it. Vladimir looks at the bracelet. It is beautiful. His wife Elena would love it. The man only wants $50 for it. Vladimir knows that it is worth more than $50. Should he buy the gold bracelet from the stranger at the bus stop? Vladimir doesn't know what to do.

MOHAMMAD'S PROBLEM

Mohammad and his family came to the United States this month. They left Afghanistan with their five children because there was so much fighting in their country. They wanted to live in peace.

Their American sponsor has rented an apartment for them. They have some blankets and dishes, but they need some clothes, furniture and food. They don't have a lot of money. They have to shop carefully. What should they buy first? Where can they get good buys on food, clothes and used furniture in your city?

SITHAT'S PROBLEM

When Sithat first came to the United States, he bought a motorcycle to get around. Now he has a new car, but he needs to sell his motorcycle.

Last week he put an ad in the paper to sell the motorcycle. Several people called, but nobody came to see the motorcycle until today.

A young man came over and he likes the motorcycle. He is willing to give Sithat what he is asking for it. Unfortunately, it is Saturday and the young man can't go to the bank to get cash. He wants to write Sithat a check. Sithat is not sure if he should take a check, but he is afraid that if he doesn't, the man might not come back next week. What should he do?

KHAYKA'S PROBLEM

Khayka needed some milk and bread from the store today, but her husband was at work and she had no money. When her husband Khong came home, he gave Khayka $20 and she went shopping at the nearby supermarket.

The supermarket is always busy in the afternoon. Khayka has to wait in line. Finally it is her turn. Her bill is $3.75. The cashier puts her money in the cash register and gives Khayka $6.25 in change. Khayka knows that she should get more money. She tells the cashier that she gave him $20 but he says she gave him only $10. What can Khayka do? Who can help her get her money back?

1. PEDRO'S PROBLEM

Where are the three men?

What is the older man doing?

What are the younger men doing?

How do they feel?

What do you think they are talking about?

Read the story silently. Underline words you don't understand. Your teacher will help you with new words.

Pedro and his two younger brothers live together in a small apartment. Pedro, who is 27, works evenings as a cook in a Mexican restaurant. His brother Hector, who is 19, goes to adult school in the morning and works part-time in a fast food restaurant in the afternoon. The youngest brother Ricardo goes to high school and delivers newspapers after school. The rest of their family live in Mexico.

The brothers used to get along well, but lately Hector and Ricardo have been fighting with Pedro over his car. His brothers want to drive it all the time. Pedro lets them drive it when they go out together, but he doesn't like his brothers driving his car without him. Hector got his license three months ago and Ricardo only has a learner's permit and can't drive alone. They are not careful drivers and they like to drive fast. Pedro is worried that they will have an accident and wreck his car. He is not sure if his insurance company would pay for the damages. Pedro thinks his brothers should walk, ride their bikes or take the bus like he did when he first came to the United States. Hector and Ricardo think that this is not right, because the car just sits in front of the house every day until 4:00 P.M., when he drives it to work.

A. COMPREHENSION CHECK.

Listen to your teacher read the sentences and answer yes, no or maybe.

1. Pedro lives with his two sons.
2. Pedro has a car.
3. Pedro works part-time in a factory.
4. Pedro drives to work at 4:00 P.M.
5. Pedro and his brothers never fight about anything.
6. Pedro's brothers, Hector and Ricardo, are teenagers.
7. Hector and Ricardo have driver's licenses and cars.
8. Hector and Ricardo are careful drivers.
9. Pedro is worried about his insurance.
10. Pedro does not want his brothers to drive his car.

B. WHAT'S HAPPENING?

First answer the questions orally. Then write down the answers.

1. Who does Pedro live with?

   _____

2. How old are Pedro's brothers, Hector and Ricardo?

   _____

3. Where does Pedro work?

   _____

4. Where does Hector go to school and where does he work?

   _____

5. What does Ricardo do?

   _____

6. What have Pedro and his brothers been fighting about?

   _____

7. When did Hector get his driver's license?

   _____

8. Why can't Ricardo drive a car alone?

   _____

(Continued on next page.)

9. How do Hector and Ricardo drive?

_____

10. How does Pedro expect his brothers to get to school and work?

_____

11. Where is Pedro's car all day long?

_____

12. Why doesn't Pedro want his brothers to drive his car?

_____

C. TALK IT OVER.

Discuss the questions with your teacher and classmates. Talk about your personal experiences. Compare your country and the United States. What is the same? What is different?

1. Do you have a driver's license? How did you get your license? Who taught you to drive?

2. Did you have a license in your country? Where is it easier to get a driver's license, here or in your country?

3. How do you get to school, to work or go shopping in the United States?

4. How did you get to school, to work or go shopping in your country? Do most people in your country have cars? Do they have to buy insurance?

5. Do you have a car now? If yes, do you let other people drive your car? Who? Do you ever borrow somebody else's car?

6. Would you rather give people rides or let them drive your car? Why?

7. Do you think people who borrow cars or ask others for rides often should offer to pay some of the car expenses? If yes, which expenses: gas, insurance, repairs?

8. Do you have to get insurance before you can drive a car in your state? Does your insurance cover other people who drive your car?

9. Do you have to pay more for family members who drive the car regularly? Is the insurance for new drivers and teenage drivers higher? Why?

10. Is car insurance in some cities and states higher than in others? Why?

11. What can happen to your insurance if you have many accidents and the insurance company has to pay for the damages?

12. Would Pedro's insurance company pay if his brothers had an accident?

13. If Hector and Ricardo were your brothers would you let them drive your car? Why? Why not?

D. WHAT'S THE PROBLEM?

Tell your teacher all the problems in the story. Your teacher will list the problems on the chalkboard.

With your classmates, choose one problem you want to discuss today. Write down the problem.

_____

_____

Find some solutions to this problem. Talk about the consequences of each solution.

What can be done about the problem? Write down some possible solutions.

1. _____

   _____

2. _____

   _____

3. _____

   _____

What might happen if you do that? Write down a possible consequence of each solution.

1. _____

   _____

2. _____

   _____

3. _____

   _____

In small groups, discuss the solutions and consequences. Choose the one solution you think is best. Each group should share its solution with the class. Tell your teacher and classmates why you think this is the best solution. Can your class agree on one solution?

E. WHAT WOULD YOU DO?

Help Pedro and his brothers. You are their friend. Give them some advice. Tell them what to do. Write down what you would say to them. Who would you talk to?

_____ , I think you should _____
(name)

_____

_____

F. SPEAK UP!

Work in a small group or with a partner. Choose someone that Pedro should talk to. Should he talk to his brothers, his insurance agent, his family in Mexico or somebody else? What should he say? Write a conversation that might help Pedro and his brothers.

Pedro: _____

_____ : _____

Pedro: _____

_____ : _____

Pedro: _____

_____ : _____

G. SHARE YOUR IDEAS.

What would you say if your neighbor asked you any of the following questions about borrowing things? Would it be OK? If not, how would you tell your neighbor you didn't want to lend something?

Can I borrow a cup of sugar?
Could I use your telephone?
Can I use your car tonight?
I need to take my wife to the hospital emergency room. Can I use your car?
Is it OK if I use your ladder?
Could I borrow your red silk dress?

Can I borrow $10?
Could you lend me $1,000 for a new car?
Can I use your sewing machine?
Can I borrow your vacuum cleaner?
Could you lend me your typewriter for a week?

Share your answers with your classmates. Give reasons for your answers.

Example: I let my neighbor use my hammer, because he always returns what he borrows. Sometimes I borrow things from him too.

2. VINAI'S PROBLEM

Where are the men?

What are they looking at?

How does the young man feel?

How does the older man feel?

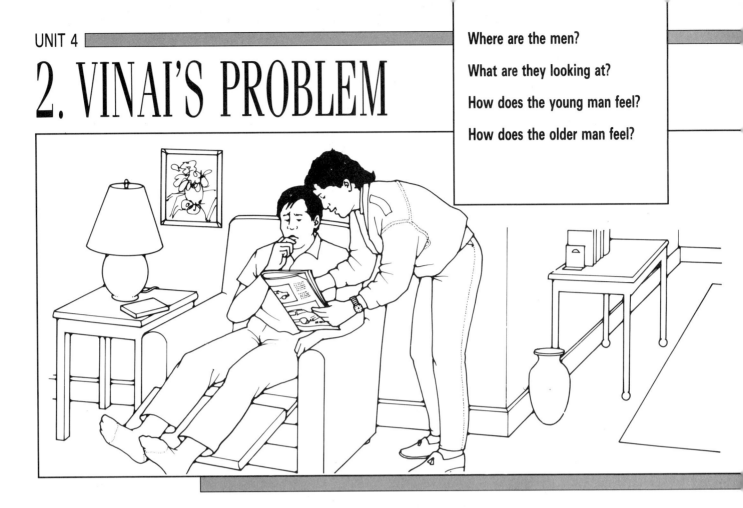

Read the dialogue silently. Underline words you don't understand. Your teacher will help you with new words.

Vinai just got hired for a new full-time job. He's very happy. He will earn $985 a month. He needs to buy a car because he will work at night and there's no bus service to his house after 10:00 P.M.

Vinai lives with his sister and brother-in-law Chanh.

Chanh: I heard the good news. You got a job.
Vinai: Yeah, I did. And guess what? I'm buying a new car.
Chanh: A new car! A new car is expensive. Buy a used car.
Vinai: But you don't need a lot of money for a new car. All you need is a down payment, then you pay a little money every month. Look at this picture of the car in the newspaper. Isn't it a great-looking car?
Chanh: How much is the down payment?
Vinai: It's only $1,200, and I have almost $2,000 in the bank.
Chanh: And how much are the monthly payments?
Vinai: Only $250.
Chanh: For how many months?
Vinai: I'm not sure, but you should see the car! It's red with a stereo and sun roof and automatic windows and air conditioning!
Chanh: But what if you lose your job? Buy a used car like I did.
Vinai: I don't want a used car like yours. It's always breaking down.

A. COMPREHENSION CHECK.

Listen to your teacher read
the sentences and answer
yes, no or maybe.

1. Vinai is sad.
2. Vinai just got a new job.
3. The job is in a factory.
4. The job is part-time.
5. Vinai will work during the day.
6. Vinai wants to buy a new car.
7. Vinai wants to buy a blue car.
8. Chanh thinks Vinai should buy a used car.
9. The down payment on the car is $1,200.
10. The monthly payments on the car are for 18 months.

B. WHAT'S HAPPENING?

First answer the questions
orally. Then write down the
answers.

1. Why is Vinai happy?

   _____

2. How much money will Vinai earn each month at his new job?

   _____

3. What time will Vinai work?

   _____

4. What time does the bus service stop going to his house?

   _____

5. What kind of car does Vinai want to buy?

   _____

6. What kind of car does Chanh think Vinai should buy?

   _____

7. How much money does Vinai have saved?

   _____

8. How much are the monthly payments on the new car?

_____

9. Does Vinai know how many months he needs to make payments on the new car?

_____

10. Why does Vinai like the new car so much?

_____

C. TALK IT OVER.

Discuss the questions with your teacher and classmates. Talk about your personal experiences. Compare your country and the United States. What is the same? What is different?

1. Do most people in your country have a car? If not, what's the most common transportation?

2. Is it necessary to have a car in your country?

3. Why do so many people in the United States have cars? Is it necessary to have a car in the United States?

4. Do you own a car? If yes, did you buy it new or used?

5. How did you find your car? Who did you buy it from?

6. Describe your car. What year is it? What make? What color? How many miles are on it?

7. How did you pay for your car in the United States? How do people pay for cars in your country?

8. What's a warranty? Did your car in the United States come with a warranty? Do cars come with warranties in your country?

9. Has your car needed many repairs in the past? If yes, what kind and how much did the repairs cost?

10. Is your car in good condition now? If not, what's wrong with it? What do you do to keep your car running well?

11. Why would you want to buy a used car? Why would you want to buy a new car?

12. When you buy a car, what do you have to do before you can drive it? Are registration and insurance more expensive for a new car or a used car?

13. Can anyone get a loan to buy a car? What do you need to get a car loan?

14. What happens if you have a loan and you are late on the monthly payments?

15. What happens if you have a loan on a car and you can't make the payments because you lose your job?

16. Do you think Vinai should buy a new or used car?

D. WHAT'S THE PROBLEM?

Tell your teacher all the problems in the story. Your teacher will list the problems on the chalkboard.

With your classmates, choose one problem you want to discuss today. Write down the problem.

_____

_____

Find some solutions to this problem. Talk about the consequences of each solution.

What can be done about the problem? Write down some possible solutions.

1. _____
   _____

2. _____
   _____

3. _____
   _____

What might happen if you do that? Write down a possible consequence of each solution.

1. _____
   _____

2. _____
   _____

3. _____
   _____

In small groups, discuss the solutions and consequences. Choose the one solution you think is best. Each group should share its solution with the class. Tell your teacher and classmates why you think this is the best solution. Can your class agree on one solution?

E. WHAT WOULD YOU DO?

Help Vinai. You are his friend. Give him some advice. Tell Vinai what to do. Write down what you would say to him.

Vinai, I think you should _____

_____

_____

F. SPEAK UP!

Work in a small group or with a partner. Choose someone that Vinai should talk to. Should he talk to Chanh, a person at the bank, the car dealer or somebody else? What should he say? Write a conversation that might help Vinai.

Vinai: _____

_____ : _____

Vinai: _____

_____ : _____

Vinai: _____

_____ : _____

G. SHARE YOUR IDEAS.

You need to buy a car. You know what model of car you want. A friend is selling the model you want. There's also an ad in the paper for the same kind of car. A car dealer has a new and a used car of that type too. Which way is the best way for you to buy the car? Read the descriptions below and decide which car you're going to buy.

1. Your friend's car is 7 years old. He wants $2,500 cash.
2. The car in the newspaper is 6 years old and costs $3,000 cash.
3. A dealer is selling a 4-year-old car. The dealer wants $3,900 cash or $900 down and $300 monthly for 1 year. It has a 6-month warranty on the engine.
4. The car dealer also has a new model available for $1,000 down and $260 a month for 3 years. It has a 12-month or 12,000-mile warranty, whichever comes first.

Give reasons for your choice. Share your answers with your classmates.

3. MARIO'S PROBLEM

Where are the three people?

How does the man in the tuxedo feel?

How do the other two people feel?

What does the older man have in his right hand?

Read the story silently. Underline words you don't understand. Your teacher will help you with new words.

Mario is a very happy father. His daughter got married today. It was a beautiful wedding and Mario invited over 200 people to the wedding, including Javier, the manager of Mario's company, and Patricia, a friend from work

After the wedding ceremony the guests went to a nice restaurant to eat. They drank and danced all night. Everyone had a good time.

It is midnight now and people are saying goodbye and leaving. Javier and Patricia are getting ready to leave too. Javier has his car keys in his hand and plans to drive Patricia home. Mario is worried because both Javier and Patricia had a lot of drinks today and are quickly finishing their last drinks now. Mario doesn't want them to drive home, but he doesn't know what to do. Javier is an important man in Mario's company and Mario doesn't want to make him angry.

A. COMPREHENSION CHECK.

Listen to your teacher read the sentences and answer yes, no or maybe.

1. Mario is sad.
2. Mario's son got married.
3. The ceremony was in a church.
4. After the ceremony the guests went to Mario's house.
5. Mario invited just a few people.
6. Mario invited the manager of his company.
7. Javier and Patricia had too much to drink.
8. Javier and Patricia are planning to walk home.
9. Javier is planning to drive home.
10. Mario is worried about Javier and Patricia.

B. WHAT'S HAPPENING?

First answer the questions orally. Then write down the answers.

1. Who got married?

   _____

2. How many people were invited to the wedding?

   _____

3. How does Mario feel about his daughter's marriage?

   _____

4. Who are Javier and Patricia?

   _____

5. Where did Javier, Patricia and the other guests go after the ceremony?

   _____

6. What did the guests do?

   _____

7. When did the guests start leaving?

   _____

(Continued on next page.)

8. How are Javier and Patricia planning on going home?

_____

9. How much did Javier and Patricia drink?

_____

10. Why is Mario worried?

_____

C. TALK IT OVER.

Discuss the questions with your teacher and classmates. Talk about your personal experiences. Compare your country and the United States. What is the same? What is different?

1. What do people from your country do at a wedding? Describe a wedding. Is there a party after the ceremony? What do you drink? What do you eat?

2. What other kinds of parties do you go to? Do people eat and drink a lot? What do they drink? How much do they drink?

3. Do you sometimes give a party? If yes, what kinds of food do you serve at your parties? When do you serve the food?

4. What kinds of drinks do you serve? Do you measure the alcohol? How?

5. Is it better to serve drinks at the beginning of the party or at the end of the party? Why? Is it better to serve drinks with food or alone? Why?

6. What happens if people drink at your home, and then drive and have an accident? Who is responsible?

7. Can children and teenagers drink in your country? Is it legal in your state to serve drinks to minors (people under 21 years old)?

8. How do you usually get to a party? If you go in a car, should the driver drink?

9. Do you ever drive home with someone who has been drinking? What could happen?

10. Can you have an open bottle of beer, wine or any other kind of alcohol in your car in your state? In your country?

11. What happens to people in the United States when the police stop them for drinking and driving? What happens in your country?

12. What does the saying, ''Friends don't let friends drive drunk'' mean?

D. WHAT'S THE PROBLEM?

Tell your teacher all the problems in the story. Your teacher will list the problems on the chalkboard.

With your classmates, choose one problem you want to discuss today. Write down the problem.

_____

_____

Find some solutions to this problem. Talk about the consequences of each solution.

What can be done about the problem? Write down some possible solutions.

1. _____

   _____

2. _____

   _____

3. _____

   _____

What might happen if you do that? Write down a possible consequence of each solution.

1. _____

   _____

2. _____

   _____

3. _____

   _____

In small groups, discuss the solutions and consequences. Choose the one solution you think is best. Each group should share its solution with the class. Tell your teacher and classmates why you think this is the best solution. Can your class agree on one solution?

E. WHAT WOULD YOU DO?

Help Mario. You are his friend. Give him some advice. Tell Mario what to do. Write down what you would say to him.

Mario, I think you should _____

_____

F. SPEAK UP!

Work in a small group or with a partner. Choose someone that Mario should talk to. Should he talk to Javier, or Patricia or somebody else? What should he say? Write a conversation that might help Mario.

Mario: _____

_____ : _____

Mario: _____

_____ : _____

Mario: _____

_____ : _____

G. SHARE YOUR IDEAS.

Cars can make our lives better, but cars can be dangerous too. Interview a driver in your class. Ask the questions. Put a check (✓) under *yes* or *no*.

	Yes	No
1. Do you wear a seat belt?		
2. Do you put a baby in a safety seat?		
3. Do you drive carefully?		
4. Do you use your turn signal when you change lanes?		
5. Does your car have good brakes?		
6. Do you drive slowly when it's raining?		
7. Do you drive over the speed limit?		
8. Do you drink and drive?		
9. Do you drive after taking medicine that makes you sleepy?		
10. Do you eat and drive?		
11. Do you smoke and drive?		
12. Do you drive when you are tired?		

Share your answers with your classmates. Is the person you interviewed a good driver? Why or why not?

MORE PROBLEMS

URSULA'S PROBLEM

Ursula is having car problems this week. Her engine is making a terrible noise, and she is afraid to drive her car. She knows that she has to take her car to a repair shop, but she doesn't know where she can find a good and honest mechanic.

The last time that she had car problems, she went to a garage near her house. The mechanic told her that the repairs would cost about $130. When she picked up her car, the mechanic asked for $230. He said something about parts and labor that Ursula didn't understand. Ursula paid him the money, but she was angry. She thought the mechanic had charged her more because she was a single woman and didn't know much about cars.

Now she is worried. Where can she find a good and honest mechanic? How can she be sure that the mechanic will not "fix" things that don't need to be fixed and charge her more money? What can she do?

BELAY'S PROBLEM

Belay wants to get a job and work. He has trouble finding a job, because he does not know how to drive and he does not have a car. Most of the good job openings are on the night shift. Unfortunately, the city buses don't run after 11:00 P.M.

Belay is getting welfare now and is going to school to learn English. He gets just enough money every month for food and rent, but not enough to pay for driving lessons or to save money for a car.

If he had a job, he could take driving lessons, save money and buy a car. But it seems that it is impossible to get a job if you don't have transportation. What do other people do?

HUMBERTO'S PROBLEM

Humberto parks his new car in front of his apartment building every night. It's his first new car and he loves it. He had saved his money for a long time until he finally had enough money to buy the car. He even took pictures of it and sent them to his family in Mexico. The car is a dream come true.

But now he is worried. Last week two cars were stolen in his neighborhood and the police were not able to find them. They were new cars like his. Humberto can hardly sleep at night now. Every time he hears a noise outside, he runs to the window to make sure that his car is still there. He has nightmares about people stealing his new car. He wakes up tired in the morning.

What can he do? How can he protect his car from thieves and get a good night's sleep again?

MINIA AND HADERA'S PROBLEM

Minia and Hadera are good friends and roommates. Their families are still in Ethiopia, but they are glad that they were able to come to the United States.

Today was a beautiful day and they took the bus to the beach. It was a one-hour trip, but they had fun. They swam in the ocean, played ball in the sand, walked on the beach and watched all the other people who were enjoying themselves. They had planned on going home in the afternoon, but they stayed to watch the beautiful sunset. They got hungry and had some pizza at a small restaurant. They saved enough money for the bus ride home.

They went to the bus stop about 8:00 P.M. and waited for the bus. They waited for more than 30 minutes, but the bus didn't come. So they asked a clerk at a nearby store about the bus, and he told them that the last bus had left about an hour ago. There would not be another bus to the city tonight. The next bus would come tomorrow morning at 8:00.

Minia and Hadera are upset. They are 35 miles from home. It is dark outside. They are frightened. What are they going to do now?

SAID'S PROBLEM

Said had to go to the drugstore tonight to get some medicine for his sick baby daughter. It was a dark and rainy night, and he parked his car in a small parking space near the store.

When he was leaving, he was in a hurry. He backed his car out of the parking space, and he hit the sportscar that was parked next to him. Said got out of the car and looked at his car. He was glad that there was not much damage. But when he looked at the other car, he saw that it had a big dent on the side.

Said is standing in the rain now. There is nobody in the parking lot. He needs to get home with the medicine. He can't wait here all night. Where is the owner of the car? What can Said do?

1. SOMSACK AND SY'S PROBLEM

Where are these people?

How does the man feel?

What is he doing?

What are the children doing?

What is the woman doing?

How does she feel?

Read the story silently. Underline words you don't understand. Your teacher will help you with new words.

Somsack was an important man in his country. He came from a rich and powerful family. Somsack and other members of his family were leaders in the government. He and his wife Sy and their children lived in a beautiful house with many servants. Then the war came. Somsack and his family were lucky to get out, but they couldn't take anything with them, not even their money.

They came to the United States eight years ago, and Somsack tried to find a job. But he couldn't find one that paid enough to support his wife and six children. They had to stay on welfare and live in a small apartment. This made Somsack feel terrible because he couldn't support his family. He became depressed and nervous. He couldn't sleep. He didn't leave the house anymore. He started drinking because it helped him forget his troubles and helped him sleep.

Sy is worried about her husband now. He is not the same man that she married. In their country he worked hard, played with the children and was a wonderful husband. Now he doesn't speak to anybody, is angry most of the time and beats the children. Last week Sy asked him not to drink anymore. Somsack got very angry and almost hit her, too. Everyone is afraid of him now.

A. COMPREHENSION CHECK.

Listen to your teacher read the sentences and answer yes, no or maybe.

1. Somsack had an important job in his country.
2. Somsack's family had a lot of money.
3. Somsack lived with his father and mother.
4. There was a war in Somsack's country.
5. Somsack brought his money from his country.
6. Somsack and his wife and children live in a big house now.
7. Somsack didn't want to get a job in the United States.
8. He is happy in the United States.
9. He drinks a lot.
10. Somsack is still a good husband and father.

B. WHAT'S HAPPENING?

First answer the questions orally. Then write down the answers.

1. Where did Somsack work in his country?

_____

2. What kind of family did Somsack come from?

_____

3. What kind of home did Somsack live in in his country?

_____

4. Why did Somsack and his family leave their country?

_____

5. What did they take with them when they left?

_____

6. What kind of home do they live in now?

_____

7. Why didn't Somsack get a job when he came to the United States?

_____

8. How did Somsack feel when he couldn't get a job?

_____

9. Where does the family get money for food, rent and other things?

_____

10. Why did Somsack start drinking?

_____

11. What kind of man was Somsack when he lived in his country?

_____

12. What kind of man is Somsack now?

_____

C. TALK IT OVER.

Discuss the questions with your teacher and classmates. Talk about your personal experiences. Compare your country and the United States. What is the same? What is different?

1. Is your life better here in the United States or was it better in your country? What is better? What is worse?

2. What did you do in your country? Can you get the same job here? If not, how do you feel about that?

3. How do you feel most of the time? Do you feel happy, sad, depressed or angry? What do you do if you feel depressed or angry?

4. Do you talk to other people about your problems? If yes, who do you talk to? How do you feel after you talk to them?

5. Do you think many people feel angry and depressed like Somsack? If yes, why?

6. Do you think it is easier for husbands or wives to get used to a new country? Is it easier for single men or married men? Single women or married women? Younger people or older people? Why?

7. Do you know anyone who drinks too much? How much is "too much"?

8. Why do people start drinking too much?

9. What are alcoholics (people with drinking problems) like? Do you want to live, work or drive with someone who drinks too much? Why not?

10. What happens to families where the father, mother or children have drinking problems?

11. What kind of health problems do alcoholics often have?

12. If people drink too much and become alcoholics, is it easy to stop drinking? What do alcohol and drug treatment centers do? Can they help alcoholics? How? What can the family and friends do to help them?

13. Do you think alcoholism is a small or a big problem in the United States? What about in your country? Is it a big problem there? What do you do about this problem in your country? Would you do the same thing here?

D. WHAT'S THE PROBLEM?

Tell your teacher all the problems in the story. Your teacher will list the problems on the chalkboard.

With your classmates, choose one problem you want to discuss today. Write down the problem.

_____

_____

Find some solutions to this problem. Talk about the consequences of each solution.

What can be done about the problem? Write down some possible solutions.

1. _____

   _____

2. _____

   _____

3. _____

   _____

What might happen if you do that? Write down a possible consequence of each solution.

1. _____

   _____

2. _____

   _____

3. _____

   _____

In small groups, discuss the solutions and consequences. Choose the one solution you think is best. Each group should share its solution with the class. Tell your teacher and classmates why you think this is the best solution. Can your class agree on one solution?

E. WHAT WOULD YOU DO?

Help Somsack and Sy. You are their friend. Give them some advice. Tell Somsack and Sy what to do. Write down what you would say to them. Would you talk to both of them or to just one of them? Who would you talk to?

_____ , I think you should _____
(name)

_____

F. SPEAK UP!

Work in a small group or with a partner. Choose someone that Somsack and Sy should talk to. Should they talk to each other, a friend, a doctor, a counselor or somebody else? What should they say? Write a conversation that might help Somsack and Sy.

_____ : _____

_____ : _____

_____ : _____

_____ : _____

_____ : _____

_____ : _____

G. SHARE YOUR IDEAS.

1. What would you do if a person in your family or one of your friends had drug or alcohol addiction problems? Look at the choices. Circle what you would do. Underline what you might do. Cross out what you would not do.

   1. Talk to them about the problem.

   2. Tell them how you feel about the problem.

   3. Ask them if you can help.

   4. Tell them to change immediately.

   5. Leave them if they don't change immediately.

   6. Keep them at home. Don't let them go out.

   7. Throw out all their drugs or liquor.

   8. Take away their money so that they can't buy any more drugs or alcohol.

   9. Tell them that you will call the police.

   10. Call the police.

   11. Watch them every minute.

   12. Don't let them see their friends.

(Continued on next page.)

13. Ask them to go to a counselor.

14. Tell them to go to a treatment center for help.

15. Offer to take them to a treatment center.

16. Tell them about the dangers and health problems.

17. Call your family doctor for help and information.

18. Anything else?

Share your answers with your classmates. Give reasons for your choices.

2. Look up *alcoholism* in the yellow pages of your telephone book.

1. Are there any treatment centers in your area? List three centers.

Name	Address	Phone Number
_____	_____	_____
_____	_____	_____
_____	_____	_____

2. Is there an alcohol abuse helpline in your area? If yes, write down the telephone number.

_____

3. Is there an Alcoholics Anonymous office in your area where you can get help and information about drinking problems? If yes, write down the telephone number.

_____

4. Write down the name and telephone number of your family doctor or a health clinic in your area.

_____

2. THE RODRIGUEZ' PROBLEM

Where are the three people?

What are they doing?

How do they feel?

What is the girl doing?

Read the story silently. Underline words you don't understand. Your teacher will help you with new words.

Every night there is fighting at the dinner table. Ten-year-old Martha Rodriguez doesn't want to eat dinner. Sometimes she eats a few vegetables but she won't eat meat. Her mother Roxanna wants Martha to eat her vegetables and meat. Roxanna says Martha is sick so much because she doesn't eat right. Cesar, Martha's father, wants peace and quiet at the dinner table. He says children will eat when they are hungry and you can't make them eat. Tonight the Rodriguez family is having another argument.

Roxanna: Don't play with your food.
Martha: I don't like broccoli. And if I eat this meat, I'll throw up.
Roxanna: It's good for you Martha.
Martha: I'm not hungry.
Roxanna: She had some cookies and soda at her friend's house an hour ago.
Cesar: Again? How many times do I have to tell you? No junk food before dinner.
Martha: But I'm hungry when I come home from school.

Roxanna doesn't understand why her daughter doesn't want to eat. When Roxanna was young she and her brothers were happy to have a hot meal. They ate what was put in front of them and they were seldom sick.

A. COMPREHENSION CHECK.

Listen to your teacher read the sentences and answer yes, no or maybe.

1. The Rodriguez family never screams and argues.
2. There are many children in the Rodriguez family.
3. Martha is in high school.
4. Martha is a healthy child.
5. Martha doesn't want to eat dinner.
6. Her mother Roxanna gives her cookies and soda after school.
7. Martha likes meat.
8. Martha isn't hungry at dinner time.
9. Martha is very hungry after school.
10. Roxanna and her brothers were always sick.

B. WHAT'S HAPPENING?

First answer the questions orally. Then write down the answers.

1. What happens every night in the Rodriguez house?

   _____

2. How many children are in the Rodriguez family?

   _____

3. What does Roxanna want her daughter to eat?

   _____

4. Why does Roxanna think Martha is sick so much?

   _____

5. What does Cesar want at the dinner table?

   _____

6. Why does Cesar think fighting at the dinner table won't help Martha eat better?

   _____

7. Why isn't Martha hungry for dinner?

   _____

8. When is Martha hungry?

   _____

9. What was Roxanna happy to have when she was young?

_____

10. Was Roxanna healthier as a child than her daughter is?

_____

C. TALK IT OVER.

Discuss the questions with your teacher and classmates. Talk about your personal experiences. Compare your country and the United States. What is the same? What is different?

1. What kind of food did you eat when you were young? Were you able to buy or get junk food (candy, cookies, soda, etc.) in your country?

2. Did you have enough food to eat in your country?

3. What did you eat for breakfast, lunch and dinner in your country? What do you eat for breakfast, lunch and dinner in the United States? Do you eat the same foods here as in your country?

4. How many servings of fruits and vegetables do you eat every day? How many servings of cereal and bread do you eat every day? How many servings of meat, fish or beans do you eat every day? How many servings of dairy products (milk, cheese, yogurt, etc.) do you eat every day?

5. Are you eating a balanced diet?

6. Did you gain or lose weight after you moved to the United States? Why?

7. Were you and your family healthier in your country or are you healthier here? Why?

8. Do meats, fruits, vegetables and breads taste the same in the United States as in your country?

9. Does the water taste the same? How much water do you drink every day? Is water good for you?

10. Do you cook for your family? If yes, how do you feel when your family won't eat what you cook? What do you do?

11. If you have children, what kind of food do they like? Are they good eaters or bad eaters?

12. If you have childen, is it difficult or easy to get them to eat foods that are good for them?

13. If your children won't eat vegetables or meats, what can you give them?

14. Are your children strong and healthy? What kinds of illnesses have they had? How do you think illnesses can be prevented?

D. WHAT'S THE PROBLEM?

Tell your teacher all the problems in the story. Your teacher will list the problems on the chalkboard.

With your classmates, choose one problem you want to discuss today. Write down the problem.

_____

_____

Find some solutions to this problem. Talk about the consequences of each solution.

What can be done about the problem? Write down some possible solutions.

1. _____

   _____

2. _____

   _____

3. _____

   _____

What might happen if you do that? Write down a possible consequence of each solution.

1. _____

   _____

2. _____

   _____

3. _____

   _____

In small groups, discuss the solutions and consequences. Choose the one solution you think is best. Each group should share its solution with the class. Tell your teacher and classmates why you think this is the best solution. Can your class agree on one solution?

E. WHAT WOULD YOU DO?

Help the Rodriguez family. You are their friend. Give them some advice. Tell the Rodriguez family what to do. Write down what you would say to them. Would you talk to all of them or just one of them? Who would you talk to?

_____ , I think you should _____
(name)

_____

F. SPEAK UP!

Work in a small group or with a partner. Choose someone that Roxanna, Cesar or Martha should talk to. Should they talk to each other, a friend, a neighbor, a relative or somebody else? What should they say? Write a conversation that might help the Rodriguez family.

_____ : _____

_____ : _____

_____ : _____

_____ : _____

_____ : _____

_____ : _____

G. SHARE YOUR IDEAS.

Look at the two lists of food below. Choose and circle the food that you think is healthier.

	List A	List B
1.	orange juice	orange drink
2.	regular milk	chocolate milk
3.	butter	margarine
4.	white bread	whole wheat bread
5.	fresh fruit	canned fruit
6.	canned soup	homemade soup
7.	peeled apple	apple with skin
8.	brown rice	white rice
9.	potato chips	baked potato
10.	soda	milk
11.	regular coffee	decaffeinated coffee
12.	herbal tea	regular tea
13.	fresh fish	pork
14.	beef	chicken
15.	cereal with sugar	cereal without sugar
16.	vegetable oil	lard

Share your answers with your classmates. Give reasons for your choices.

3. ANITA AND CARLOS' PROBLEM

Where are the man and the woman?

What is the woman doing?

How does she feel?

What is the man doing?

Read the story silently. Underline words you don't understand. Your teacher will help you with new words.

Anita and her husband Carlos have good news and bad news. The good news is that Anita is pregnant for the first time and Carlos just got a full-time job last week. They both will get free medical insurance with his new job.

The bad news is that the insurance will start in six months, but Anita is already four months pregnant. The baby will be born before the insurance starts. They're worried because they don't have enough money saved to pay the hospital. Hospitals and doctors are very expensive.

Money is tight because Anita and Carlos had to buy a car so Carlos could get to work. They have car payments now. Rent is high in their city, and by the time they pay off their bills, there is no money left to save. Anita works part-time now and her paycheck also helps pay for everything. But she can't depend on her job. She thinks her boss will lay her off when he finds out that she is pregnant.

A. COMPREHENSION CHECK.

Listen to your teacher read the sentences and answer yes, no or maybe.

1. Anita is pregnant for the second time.
2. Carlos just got a full-time job.
3. The job is in a factory.
4. Only Carlos will get insurance from his job.
5. Anita and Carlos have to pay for the insurance.
6. Anita is four months pregnant.
7. Anita goes to a clinic for prenatal care.
8. Anita and Carlos have car payments.
9. Anita works part-time.
10. Anita's boss might lay her off.

B. WHAT'S HAPPENING?

First answer the questions orally. Then write down the answers.

1. How many children do Carlos and Anita have?

   _____

2. When did Carlos get his job?

   _____

3. When does the medical insurance begin for Anita and Carlos?

   _____

4. When will Anita have her baby?

   _____

5. Why are they worried?

   _____

6. Does Anita work full-time?

   _____

7. Why did they buy a car?

   _____

8. Is their rent cheap or expensive?

   _____

(Continued on next page.)

9. Why can't they save money?

_____

10. Why can't Anita depend on her job?

_____

C. TALK IT OVER.

Discuss the questions with your teacher and classmates. Talk about your personal experiences. Compare your country and the United States. What is the same? What is different?

1. Where were you born? In a house, a hospital or someplace else?
2. Did a doctor, nurse, midwife or someone else help with the birth?
3. Where do most women give birth in your country? Where do most women give birth in the United States?
4. When should a pregnant woman start seeing a midwife, nurse or doctor for prenatal care? Why?
5. Do you have medical insurance? If you do, how much do you pay for it? Is it full (100 percent) coverage or less?
6. If you don't have medical insurance, what do you do when you need to see a nurse or doctor? How much do you pay for it?
7. Did you have medical insurance in your country? If you did, how much was it? If you didn't have medical insurance, what did you do when you needed to see a doctor or nurse? How did you pay for it?
8. Is it expensive to get medical care in your country? How do poor people get medical care in your country?
9. Do you think medical care is expensive in the United States? Why?
10. Do you know anyone in the United States who was sick or pregnant and didn't have medical insurance? What did they do?
11. Can pregnant women get medical care if they don't have insurance or enough money to pay for the hospital? If yes, how?
12. Do you think medical and dental care should be free for everyone? Why or why not?
13. If Anita is doing her job well, can her boss fire her because she's pregnant? Are there laws to protect women? What are they?

D. WHAT'S THE PROBLEM?

Tell your teacher all the problems in the story. Your teacher will list the problems on the chalkboard.

With your classmates, choose one problem you want to discuss today. Write down the problem.

_____

_____

Find some solutions to this problem. Talk about the consequences of each solution.

What can be done about the problem? Write down some possible solutions.	What might happen if you do that? Write down a possible consequence of each solution.
1. _____ _____	1. _____ _____
2. _____ _____	2. _____ _____
3. _____ _____	3. _____ _____

In small groups, discuss the solutions and consequences. Choose the one solution you think is best. Each group should share its solution with the class. Tell your teacher and classmates why you think this is the best solution. Can your class agree on one solution?

E. WHAT WOULD YOU DO?

Help Anita and Carlos. You are their friend. Give them some advice. Tell Anita and Carlos what to do. Write down what you would say to them. Would you talk to both of them or just one of them? Who would you talk to?

_____ , I think you should _____
(name)

_____

_____

F. SPEAK UP!

Work in a small group or with a partner. Choose someone that Anita and Carlos should talk to. Should they talk to each other, a friend, a hospital administrator, a midwife or somebody else? What should they say? Write a conversation that might help Anita and Carlos.

_____ : _____

_____ : _____

_____ : _____

_____ : _____

_____ : _____

_____ : _____

G. SHARE YOUR IDEAS.

Prenatal care is very important for pregnant women. What is healthy and what is unhealthy for pregnant women to do? Look at the list below and check what is healthy and what is unhealthy.

	Healthy	Unhealthy
1. Eating a balanced diet (fruits, vegetables, meat, fish, milk, bread)		
2. Smoking		
3. Drinking alcohol		
4. Drinking diet soda		
5. Exercising		
6. Getting regular checkups		
7. Seeing a doctor, nurse or midwife early in pregnancy		
8. Eating junk food		
9. Drinking a lot of milk		
10. Taking over-the-counter medication		
11. Lifting heavy things		
12. Wearing high heels		
13. Eating a lot of salt		
14. Gaining 25 pounds during pregnancy		
15. Gaining 60 pounds during pregnancy		

Share your answers with your classmates. Give reasons for your answers.

MORE PROBLEMS

HENG'S PROBLEM

Heng came to the United States 10 years ago. In his country he was a teacher. Now he wants to work for the sheriff's department as a correctional officer. He went to school, studied hard and passed the written and oral tests. Then he applied for a job.

Before Heng could be hired, he had to have a physical examination. The news was not good. The report said that he was overweight, out of shape and that his cholesterol was too high. Heng was upset. He had worked so hard to pass all of the tests, and now he couldn't get the job. Is there anything that he can do?

DAMIANA'S PROBLEM

Damiana and her husband work on farms. They pick fruit, nuts and vegetables. It's hard work, but they are used to the work. In Mexico they both grew up on farms. They like the work, because the family can work together, and they can earn more money if they work fast. This summer their older daughters will help with the harvest.

Last week Damiana's boss sprayed the fields with a pesticide. Damiana is worried. She doesn't want to get sick like she did last year. She had headaches, was dizzy and vomited. Many of her friends were sick, too. The boss said that this had nothing to do with the spraying. The spraying was safe. He said that they must have all had the flu. What can she do? How can she be sure that she and her family will be safe? They can't quit their jobs, because they need the money for their living expenses.

VINCENT'S PROBLEM

Vincent's wife died three years ago and he is now raising his two children by himself. His daughter is 8 years old and his son is 10. Vincent works in a restaurant. It's a small restaurant and he is the only cook. He works the breakfast and lunch shifts and gets home when his children get out of school. He is off on weekends, so he doesn't need a baby-sitter.

Last night his little daughter was up all night coughing, sneezing and vomiting. She is still sick this morning, but she isn't vomiting anymore. Vincent has to go to work. What should he do with his daughter? Should he send her to school, take her to work with him or leave her home alone? It's hard to be a single parent.

BOSY'S PROBLEM

Bosy's daughter Mira has a sore throat and a high fever. Bosy took her to the doctor, and the doctor gave her some medicine. Bosy's mother-in-law came over today to baby-sit for little Mira while Bosy and her husband went to work.

While Bosy was at work, her mother-in-law cooked some herbs and made Mira drink the juices. They made Mira dizzy. Then the mother-in-law put lots of blankets on Mira to make her sweat out the fever. She didn't give her the medicine from the doctor, because she thought the medicines from her country were much better. They had always helped her own children.

When Bosy came home from work she was very upset. Mira's fever was very, very high. What kind of herbs had her mother-in-law given Mira? Should Bosy give her the American medicine now? Should she call the doctor? What should she do?

JULIA'S PROBLEM

Two years ago, before Julia met and married her husband, she had lived with another man. She left him because he would not stop taking drugs. It was a bad time in her life and she never told her husband about this man.

Yesterday she met an old friend in a store. This friend said that Julia's old boyfriend has AIDS. She asked Julia if she was OK.

Julia is feeling fine now, but she is worried that she might not stay healthy. Did her old boyfriend already have AIDS when they lived together or did he get AIDS after they broke up? Could she have AIDS and not know it? How do people know that they have AIDS? How could she find out for sure without telling her husband about this man? If she goes and sees a doctor will the doctor tell her husband why she came to see him? What can she do?

1. ANH AND TONG'S PROBLEM

Where is the woman?

What time is it?

What is she doing?

How does she feel?

Read the story silently. Underline words you don't understand. Your teacher will help you with new words.

Anh is a young housewife with two children. She and her husband Tong came to the United States four years ago. Tong is an assembler in a factory. He works hard and takes good care of his family. Sometimes he works seven days a week and he comes home very tired.

Anh has a lot of free time. The children go to school and they don't come home for lunch. Anh cooks breakfast and dinner. She cleans their small apartment, washes clothes in a washing machine and she watches a lot of TV. Anh used to visit her friends and neighbors, but many are working now and some have moved away. She wants to go out on weekends, but Tong doesn't want to because he is working or he is too tired. Anh is lonely and bored.

Anh wants to learn to drive and wants to work. When she talks to Tong about this he gets angry. He doesn't have time to teach Anh to drive. He doesn't want to buy a second car. And he doesn't want Anh to work. He thinks a wife should stay at home and take care of the children while the husband goes to work.

A. COMPREHENSION CHECK.

Listen to your teacher read the sentences and answer yes, no or maybe.

1. Anh and Tong have many children.
2. Anh and Tong came to the United States last year.
3. They came from Laos.
4. The children stay home all day.
5. Tong works part-time.
6. Anh has a lot of free time.
7. Anh wants to stay home on weekends.
8. Anh is happy.
9. Anh wants to learn how to drive.
10. Tong wants to buy a new car.
11. Tong thinks women should stay at home.

B. WHAT'S HAPPENING?

First answer the questions orally. Then write down the answers.

1. When did Anh and Tong come to the United States?

   _____

2. How many children do they have?

   _____

3. What do the children do every day?

   _____

4. How many days a week does Tong work?

   _____

5. What does Anh do every day?

   _____

6. Where are Anh's friends and neighbors?

   _____

7. What does Anh want to do on weekends?

   _____

8. What does Tong want to do on weekends?

   _____

9. What does Anh want Tong to teach her?

_____

10. Why does Anh want to go to work?

_____

11. Why does Tong get angry?

_____

C. TALK IT OVER.

Discuss the questions with your teacher and classmates. Talk about your personal experiences. Compare your country and the United States. What is the same? What is different?

1. Where do you have more free time, in your country or in the United States? Why? Are you sometimes lonely or bored in the United States? Why?

2. Do you have friends in the United States? If yes, where did you meet your friends? What do you and your friends do together?

3. Did you have many friends in your country? Where did you meet them? What did you do together?

4. Do you know how to drive? Is it important to know how to drive in your country? Why? Why not? Do many women drive in your country? Is it important to know how to drive in the United States? Why? Should women also know how to drive? Why?

5. Who can teach you to drive in the United States? Do you know anyone who has gone to a driving school? Look in the yellow pages. What's the name of a driving school in your city? _____ How much do driving lessons cost? _____

6. Do many women have jobs in your country? What kinds of jobs do women have in your country? Do most women in your country do their own housework or do they pay someone else to do it?

7. What jobs do women have in the United States? Why do so many women in the United States work? Do most women in the United States do their own housework or do they pay someone else to do it?

8. Do men from your country like their wives to have jobs outside the home? Why? Why not? Do some married women from your country now have jobs in the United States? Do they like their jobs? Why? Why not? Who takes care of their children while they work? How do you feel about working mothers?

9. Do you think women with pre-school children (children under 5 years) should stay at home or go to work? Do many American women with young children work? Who takes care of their children and the housework?

10. What's a child-care center? Look in the yellow pages of the telephone book under Child-Care Centers. Is there one near your house? What's the telephone number? _____ How much does a week of child care cost? _____ Is it cheaper or more expensive than paying a baby-sitter?

11. If a woman doesn't have a job because she doesn't have any training, transportation or English skills, what can she do so she isn't bored?

D. WHAT'S THE PROBLEM?

Tell your teacher all the problems in the story. Your teacher will list the problems on the chalkboard.

With your classmates, choose one problem you want to discuss today. Write down the problem.

_____

_____

Find some solutions to this problem. Talk about the consequences of each solution.

What can be done about the problem? Write down some possible solutions.

1. _____

   _____

2. _____

   _____

3. _____

   _____

What might happen if you do that? Write down a possible consequence of each solution.

1. _____

   _____

2. _____

   _____

3. _____

   _____

In small groups, discuss the solutions and consequences. Choose the one solution you think is best. Each group should share its solution with the class. Tell your teacher and classmates why you think this is the best solution. Can your class agree on one solution?

E. WHAT WOULD YOU DO?

Help Anh and Tong. You are their friend. Give them some advice. Tell Anh and Tong what to do. Write down what you would say to them. Would you talk to both of them or to just one of them? Who would you talk to?

_____ , I think you should _____
(name)

_____

_____

F. SPEAK UP!

Work in a small group or with a partner. Choose someone that Anh or Tong should talk to. Should they talk to each other, their children, friends, parents, neighbors or somebody else? What should they say? Write a conversation that might help Anh and Tong.

_____ : _____

_____ : _____

_____ : _____

_____ : _____

_____ : _____

_____ : _____

G. SHARE YOUR IDEAS.

How much time do you spend on daily activities in the United States? How much time did you spend on daily activities in your country? Look at the Work Chart below and write down how many hours you spend on each activity every day. Then look at the Recreation Chart on page 100 and write down how many hours you spend on each of those activities every day. Add up the total number of hours on both charts.

WORK CHART

	Number of hours	
	In the U.S.	In your country
work at a job		
go to school		
drive/walk/take the bus to school or work		
cook		
clean		
take care of children		
do laundry		
garden		
go shopping for food/clothes		
other activities:		
Total number of hours:		

(Continued on next page.)

RECREATION CHART

	Number of hours	
	In the U.S.	In your country
watch TV		
read		
talk on the phone		
visit family or friends		
exercise/do sports		
go window shopping		
other activities:		
Total number of hours:		

Now compare the number of hours you spend on daily activities in the United States and how many hours you spent on daily activities in your country. What is the same? What is different? Share the information with your classmates. Compare the number of hours the men and women in your class spend on daily activities. For example, who spends more time on recreation, the men or the women?

2. SAID'S PROBLEM

Where are the two men?

What are they doing?

How does the man on the left feel?

Why do you think he feels that that way?

Read the dialogue silently. Underline words you don't understand. Your teacher will help you with new words.

Said has to make some difficult decisions about his future. He is 25, single, and he came to the United States last year without his family.

Said is talking to his friend Raul about his problems.

Raul: Hey, Said! What's up? You look worried.

Said: Oh, I don't know what to do.

Raul: What do you mean?

Said: Well, I don't know if I should stay in school and learn more English or get a job.

Raul: Your English is pretty good. It's better than mine.

Said: Yeah, but I don't read or write well.

Raul: What kind of job do you want?

Said: I don't know. Right now I could only get a job that wouldn't pay much, like a restaurant or a cleaning job. But I want to get a better job so that I can send money to my family. I'd really like to be a mechanic, but that takes a year or more of training.

Raul: Mechanics make good money. I don't like my job at the Burger Place. It's boring and it doesn't pay much. I'd like to get a better job, too. Maybe when my English is better, I can be a waiter.

A. COMPREHENSION CHECK.

Listen to your teacher read
the sentences and answer
yes, no or maybe.

1. Said's family is not in the United States.
2. Said is married.
3. Said is worried about his future.
4. Said knows what he wants to do.
5. Said speaks English better than his friend Raul.
6. Said can read and write well.
7. Raul works in a fast-food restaurant.
8. Said wants to work in a restaurant, too.
9. Said wants to be a taxi driver.
10. Said wants to help his family.

B. WHAT'S HAPPENING?

First answer the questions
orally. Then write down the
answers.

1. How old is Said?

   _____

2. Where is his family?

   _____

3. How long has Said been in the United States?

   _____

4. What is Said worried about?

   _____

5. How is Said's English?

   _____

6. What kind of a job could Said get now?

   _____

7. Why doesn't Said's friend Raul like his job?

   _____

8. What does Raul have to do to get a better job?

_____

9. What would Said like to be?

_____

10. How long is the training for a mechanic?

_____

C. TALK IT OVER.

Discuss the questions with your teacher and classmates. Talk about your personal experiences. Compare your country and the United States. What is the same? What is different?

1. What did you do in your country? How long did you have that job?

2. Did you have the same job as your father or mother? Do young people in your country choose their own jobs or do they usually go into their father's business or profession? Is it the same in this country or is it different? Why?

3. Do people in your country change jobs a lot or do they keep the same jobs most of their lives? What about in the United States?

4. Is it easy to move up in a job in your country or do you stay at the same level you started? What about in the United States?

5. What is _skills training_? Where do people in your country learn skills (how to become a mechanic, seamstress, barber, etc.): in a school or on the job? Is the training free or do people have to pay for it?

6. Can you get some skills training in your area now? Where? What kind of training? Is it free or do you have to pay? What skills interest you? Do you have to be able to read and write in English to take this training?

7. Do you think it is necessary for most jobs to be able to read and write in English? Why? Why not?

8. What do you think young people should get first: education/training or job experience? Can they do both at the same time? How?

9. In the United States, do people with college educations always make more money? Why? Why not? What about in your country?

10. In the United States, do only young people go to school or training classes or do older people go too? Why? What about in your country?

11. What are job or career counselors? What do they do? How can they help you if you don't know what you want to do? Do you know anyone who has gone to a job counselor? Is there one in your school or city? Where? Do you have to pay for the advice or is it free?

D. WHAT'S THE PROBLEM?

Tell your teacher all the problems in the story. Your teacher will list the problems on the chalkboard.

With your classmates, choose one problem you want to discuss today. Write down the problem.

_____

_____

Find some solutions to this problem. Talk about the consequences of each solution.

What can be done about the problem? Write down some possible solutions.

1. _____

   _____

2. _____

   _____

3. _____

   _____

What might happen if you do that? Write down a possible consequence of each solution.

1. _____

   _____

2. _____

   _____

3. _____

   _____

In small groups, discuss the solutions and consequences. Choose the one solution you think is best. Each group should share its solution with the class. Tell your teacher and classmates why you think this is the best solution. Can your class agree on one solution?

E. WHAT WOULD YOU DO?

Help Said. You are his friend. Give him some advice. Tell Said what to do. Write down what you would say to him.

Said, I think you should _____

_____

F. SPEAK UP!

Work in a small group or with a partner. Choose someone that Said should talk to. Should he talk to his teacher, a friend, a job counselor or somebody else? What should he say? Write a conversation that might help Said.

Said: _____

_____ : _____

Said: _____

_____ : _____

Said: _____

_____ : _____

G. SHARE YOUR IDEAS.

Ask a classmate these questions and write down the answers.

1. Do you know anyone who has a job? Who?

   _____

2. Where does he or she work?

   _____

3. What is he or she doing? What are his or her duties?

   _____

4. Did he or she get some training or have previous job experience for this job? If not, how did he or she learn this job?

   _____

5. How did he or she get the job (through friends, the newspapers, a job placement office or a sign in the window)?

   _____

Now look at the answers and write a story about this person.

Example: Bao's son has a job in a factory. He makes bicycle parts. He gets $6 an hour. He learned his job in this factory. His friend helped him get the job.

Read your story to your classmates. Your teacher may wish to collect the stories and share them with the class.

3. KER'S PROBLEM

What are the people in the picture doing?

Where are they?

What is the woman pointing to?

How does the man feel?

Read the story silently. Underline words you don't understand. Your teacher will help you with new words.

Sua and Ker are a young couple from Laos. They have three young children. Ker's mother lives with them and takes care of the children. Sua and Ker go to school. Ker is getting training in landscape and gardening. He was a farmer in his country and he likes to work outdoors with plants, trees and flowers. His wife Sua is studying English.

Last week Ker's teacher told him about a job in a big apartment complex. Ker went and talked to the manager. The manager needs someone to do the gardening and to clean the laundry rooms and swimming pool area. The starting wage is $5.50 an hour. The benefits are one week of paid vacation a year and health insurance after three months on the job.

Ker would like to do the gardening, but he doesn't want to clean the laundry rooms and the pool area. He isn't sure if he should take the job because he will only make $250 more a month than he and his family get from welfare payments right now. He is also worried because the health insurance won't start right away.

A. COMPREHENSION CHECK.

Listen to your teacher read the sentences and answer yes, no or maybe.

1. Sua and Ker are married.
2. Ker's father lives with them.
3. They have to pay a baby-sitter when Sua goes to school.
4. Ker is getting training in landscape and gardening.
5. Ker wants to work in a factory.
6. Ker has a chance to get a job as a gardener.
7. Ker likes to clean buildings.
8. Ker and his family are on welfare now.
9. The job pays more than welfare.
10. The health insurance will start right away.

B. WHAT'S HAPPENING?

First answer the questions orally. Then write down the answers.

1. Where are Sua and Ker from?

   _____

2. How many children do they have?

   _____

3. Who takes care of the children while Sua and Ker go to school?

   _____

4. What did Ker do in his country?

   _____

5. What kind of training is he getting now?

   _____

6. What did Ker's teacher tell him?

   _____

7. What are the job duties?

   _____

8. How does Ker feel about the job duties?

_____

9. What is the pay and what are the benefits?

_____

10. What worries Ker about taking the job?

_____

C. TALK IT OVER.

Discuss the questions with your teacher and classmates. Talk about your personal experiences. Compare your country and the United States. What is the same? What is different?

1. Are you working now? Where do you work? What are your job duties? How much is your pay? What are the benefits? Do you like everything about your job or are there some things you don't like to do? What?

2. What is welfare? Who can get welfare payments in the United States? Where does welfare money come from? How long can people stay on welfare?

3. Do you have welfare in your country? If not, what does a family do if the father or mother cannot support the family?

4. How much would a family with three children receive from welfare in your state? Do they get food stamps, housing aid and medical insurance too? Do they lose these benefits if they take a low-paying job with no benefits?

5. Does the welfare money increase every year or does it stay the same? Does the welfare money stop coming in sometimes? When? Why?

6. Why are some people who get welfare afraid to take a job and stop getting welfare money?

7. Is it easy to get jobs in your state? How much do entry-level jobs pay in your state? Can a family with three children live on that salary? Do they usually get health benefits right away? If not, what do they do?

8. If you get a job and the "starting wage" is $5.50 an hour, will it always be the same or will you get more money in a few months? What do you have to do to get a salary increase?

9. If you have a job, but you don't like your job because the pay is low or there are no benefits, what can you do?

10. What's _job experience_? How do people get job experience? Why is getting job experience important?

11. Do you think it is better to keep getting welfare payments or to take a job if a job is available? Why?

D. WHAT'S THE PROBLEM?

Tell your teacher all the problems in the story. Your teacher will list the problems on the chalkboard.

With your classmates, choose one problem you want to discuss today. Write down the problem.

_____

_____

Find some solutions to this problem. Talk about the consequences of each solution.

What can be done about the problem? Write down some possible solutions.

1. _____

   _____

2. _____

   _____

3. _____

   _____

What might happen if you do that? Write down a possible consequence of each solution.

1. _____

   _____

2. _____

   _____

3. _____

   _____

In small groups, discuss the solutions and consequences. Choose the one solution you think is best. Each group should share its solution with the class. Tell your teacher and classmates why you think this is the best solution. Can your class agree on one solution?

E. WHAT WOULD YOU DO?

Help Ker. You are his friend. Give him some advice. Tell Ker what to do. Write down what you would say to him.

Ker, I think you should _____

_____

_____

F. SPEAK UP!

Work in a small group or with a partner. Choose someone that Ker should talk to. Should he talk to his teacher, his welfare worker, his wife, his friend or somebody else? What should he say? Write a conversation that might help Ker.

Ker: _____

_____ : _____

Ker: _____

_____ : _____

Ker: _____

_____ : _____

G. SHARE YOUR IDEAS.

Look at the "Help Wanted" ads in your local newspaper. What kind of jobs are available in your city? Find some jobs that you like and fill in the information on the chart below.

After you make a list of the jobs you like, circle the one you like the best. Then get together with a classmate. Ask the questions on the next page.

Example: COOK needed. Experience or training nec. $5.25/hr. Part-time. Call 265-7173.

Job	Pay	Full/part-time	Benefits	Exper./Trng	Phone
cook	$5.25	part-time	?	yes	265-7173

Job	Pay	Full/part-time	Benefits	Exper./Trng.	Phone

1. What job do you like best?

    _____

2. How much is the pay?

    _____

3. Is it full-time or part-time?

    _____

4. Are there any benefits? What are they?

    _____

5. Do you need experience or training?

    _____

6. What's the phone number or address?

    _____

If all the information is not in the ad, call the telephone number in the ad when you get home. Ask some questions. Tell your teacher and classmates what you found out the next day.

MORE PROBLEMS

HUNG'S PROBLEM

Hung is 44 years old. He has been in this country for four years and has gone to school every day to study English. He understands everything, and he can read and write well. Unfortunately, Americans can't understand him when he tries to speak English. When they don't understand him, he gets nervous, his English gets worse and he can't speak at all.

He applied for a job as a taxi driver, but he didn't get the job. Then he applied for a job as a school bus driver and they told him that his English was not good enough to handle emergencies. Finally he got a job as a waiter, but he lost his job because the customers couldn't understand him. He is very discouraged now. What should he do? What kind of job should he look for?

UBAH'S PROBLEM

Ubah is looking for a job. Two of her friends are already working. One friend is working as a cook in a restaurant. The other friend is working as a cleaning woman in a factory. Ubah hopes that they can help her find a job.

Yesterday was a lucky day. Both of her friends called and told her to come for a job interview. The first job is a cleaning job in the factory. It pays $4.25 an hour and Ubah will get a paycheck every two weeks. The other job is in the restaurant. It is a kitchen helper job. The owner wants to pay her $4.00 an hour in cash. He says that's a good deal, because if she gets cash she will not have to pay taxes and social security.

Ubah doesn't know what to do. Is it better to work for cash or is it better to get a check and pay taxes and social security?

VLADIMIR'S PROBLEM

Vladimir has been looking in the paper for a job. He was an electronic engineer in Russia and he would like to get a job as an engineer with an American company. He was the chief engineer of his department in Russia and he has 18 years of experience.

Last week he saw an ad in the paper.

> Electronic engineer and electronic technicians needed. Experienced. Excellent salary and benefits. Call for information. Mr. Oberlin 256-7652.

Vladimir called the number, made an appointment, filled out an application and went to an interview. Finally, they called him back and told him that he could start work as an electronic technician. Another person with 12 years experience in the United States was hired for the engineer's job.

Vladimir was very disappointed. He wanted the engineer's job. What should he do? Should he take the technician job or look for another job?

SOUTTA AND PANNE'S PROBLEM

Soutta and Panne live in a large American city. They live in a small apartment with their four children. It is very noisy and crowded. They can't move into a larger apartment, because the rents are very high. It's very difficult for Panne to find a job, because his English is not very good and he doesn't have any special skills or training. He was a farmer and soldier in Laos.

Panne's cousin wants to move to a small farming town 200 miles from their city. The rents are much lower there. They could rent a three-bedroom house with a garden for the same money that they pay for a two-bedroom apartment in the city. Maybe they could even find work on the farms.

Panne's wife, Soutta, isn't sure that she wants to move. She has many friends in the city and she likes the schools. There are no Laotian people in the farming town and maybe there are no English classes either. Maybe the Americans in that small town won't like them. She is afraid to move. What should they do?